Into Battle

To my wife and our three children,
Ian, Elizabeth and Alison

Into Battle

1914–1918

Ernest Parker

Pen & Sword
MILITARY

First published in Great Britain in 2012 by
Pen & Sword Military
an imprint of
Pen & Sword Books Ltd
47 Church Street
Barnsley
South Yorkshire
S70 2AS

ISBN: 978-1-78159-155-0

Typeset in 11pt Ehrhardt by
Mac Style, Beverley, E. Yorkshire

Printed and bound in the UK by MPG Printgroup, UK

Pen & Sword Books Ltd incorporates the Imprints of Pen & Sword Aviation,
Pen & Sword Family History, Pen & Sword Maritime, Pen & Sword Military,
Pen & Sword Discovery, Wharncliffe Local History, Wharncliffe True Crime,
Wharncliffe Transport, Pen & Sword Select, Pen & Sword Military Classics,
Leo Cooper, The Praetorian Press, Remember When, Seaforth Publishing
and Frontline Publishing.

For a complete list of Pen & Sword titles please contact
PEN & SWORD BOOKS LIMITED
47 Church Street, Barnsley, South Yorkshire, S70 2AS, England
E-mail: enquiries@pen-and-sword.co.uk
Website: www.pen-and-sword.co.uk

Contents

Foreword to the First Edition

This book is the story of a soldier's pilgrimage of half a century
ago in the grimmest war ever fought by our country. It was a
pilgrimage which hundreds of thousands of young men made
from the recruiting office in Britain to the veteran's final mastery over
self in the shell-scarred, rat-haunted slime of the front line that for four
years stretched – almost unchanged – from the North Sea to the Swiss
frontier. For many that pilgrimage ended in a nameless grave in the
mud or a wooden cross in one of the cemetery gardens of northern
France and Belgium which still commemorate the courage, sacrifice
and endurance that sustained this country's resolve against the most
powerful army the world had ever seen and that won in the end, at such
terrible cost, victory.

Reading Ernest Parker's artless but deeply-moving account of his life
in the First World War, I was again and again reminded of lines in
which such poets as Robert Nichols, Wilfred Owen and Siegfried
Sassoon set down their impressions of their generation's tremendous
ordeal:

> of all borne and left unsaid
> By the soldier. By the mire
> Closing o'er a comrade's head,
> By the faces stripped by fire,
> By daylight's dumb and crowded wire,
> By moonlight's lonely, loathsome dead …

Most of all, I found myself recalling the heroes of that great, though temporarily forgotten, novel, Her Privates We* – Sergeant Tozer, Weeper Smart, Little Martlow, Shem, Madeley:

> These apparently rude and brutal natures comforted, encouraged, and reconciled each other to Fate with a tenderness and tact which was more moving than anything in life. They had nothing; not even their own bodies, which had become mere implements of warfare. They turned from the wreckage and misery of life to an empty heaven, and from an empty heaven to the silence of their own hearts. They had been brought to the last extremity of hope, and yet they put their hands on each other's shoulders and said with a passionate conviction that it would be all right, though they had faith in nothing but in themselves and in each other.

As Edmund Blunden wrote of the infantryman of that now remote war, 'It is time to hint to a new age what your value, what your love was; your Ypres is gone and you are gone; we were lucky to see you "in the pink" against white-ribbed and socket-eyed despair.' It is just this that Ernest Parker's narrative enables us to see.

Arthur Bryant

---

* By Frederic Manning, published originally (Peter Davies) under the pseudonym "Private 19022".

Preface to the First Edition

Well over thirty years ago, when the experiences of early youth were fresh in my mind, I wrote this brief narrative in the hope that one day I might wish to recall the memory of those formative years from 1914 to 1918. But for the enterprise of my son Ian, at a time when he had just finished his finals for an honours degree at Oxford, these reminiscences would never have seen the light of day. It was he who disinterred the almost illegible manuscript.

This, then, is the story of a youth of just under eighteen years of age from the time he joined Kitchener's Army as one of the first hundred thousand in 1914, until he found himself in hospital recovering from his last wound on the day of the Armistice on 11 November, 1918.

Looking back over the past half-century, the narrator, who finds he has forgotten so much of the detail of the happenings of those fateful four years, is filled with pity for his less-fortunate comrades and recalls with surprise the providential numbness by which those men he once knew so intimately were enabled to toil steadily throughout such battles as the Somme and Passchendaele without introspection or fear of the many dread tomorrows which so often were to succeed their nightly vigils.

How fortunate it was to be young then, and how very different it was to find oneself a quarter of a century later faced with another World War when wife and family as well as home and a satisfying and exciting career had to be abandoned in middle age in order to don the same old khaki serge.

It is only fitting that royalties from the sale of this book should be given to the Queen Alexandra Hospital Home at Worthing, where there are still a number of men disabled in the 1914-18 War. This worthy institution is, unfortunately, hard pressed for funds.

E. P.

Introduction to this Edition

All of them similar, no two alike; almost all of them in some degree illuminating, and therefore valuable to those who wish to form an understanding of a vast event: I am referring to the veterans' recollections of the First World War. As the decades have ticked by the volume of these has grown enormously, and obviously the quality has been variable. In general, allowing for the initial impact of shock, attributable to the peculiarly distressing novelties of the First World War, it is the earliest impressions that are most valuable. Ernest Parker's narrative, whose first publication coincided with the 50th anniversary of the outbreak of the War, was in fact composed in the early Twenties, very close to the event, in the hope, he tells us, 'that one day I might wish to recall the memory of those formative years from 1914 to 1918.'

That is a revealing statement: 'one day I might wish to recall'. An almost universal characteristic of that generation of ex-Servicemen (the demobilized Citizen Soldiers) was their wish not to recall the revolting and quite literally 'shocking' scenes which they had witnessed, particularly on the Western Front. It is probably for that reason that Parker's account is so sparse. This, indeed, is the only serious criticism that I would make of it: it could, and should, have been much longer. It is at all times lucid, precise, wonderfully descriptive: there ought to be much more of it.

However, even within the obvious restraints under which it was composed, it possesses one special degree of illumination which places it in a limited category of information sources. Ernest Parker was one of that ever-increasing number of men who rose from private soldiers through the ranks of the non-commissioned officers and the Officer Cadet Battalions to end the War as an officer, which entitled him, as you might say, to two wars for the price of one – certainly to two points of view of the thing.

Often enough, in such memoirs as this, we meet the everlastingly famished young soldier, the youthful volunteer with a boy's appetite and a boy's eternal hunger. Like so many more, both in camp in England and 'up the line' in France, he rated hunger as one of the War's chief afflictions:

> 'Alas, when we needed food most it sometimes did not arrive at all, and it was far from pleasant to spend twenty-four hours or more in the front line without anything whatever to eat … the front-line soldier was always hungry.'

Equally 'far from pleasant' were the boils and diarrhoea which followed from drinking boiled shell-hole water. And so also were the fatigues which made the soldiers' nights as beastly as their days, both in the line and out of it, and which could, he recalls, sometimes so affect the younger ones that on one occasion he 'fell into a sleep so deep that twenty-four hours passed before I awoke'. This actually happened in the front line, where it was a serious offence, so he was considerably alarmed when he awoke in an empty trench with only one comrade. However, they soon discovered their company, whereupon

> 'Our Company Sergeant (sic) spoke to us sharply, and we earned the name of "Shut-Eye Kings".'

However, lack of food, although intermittent, and constant weariness, as well as inescapable horrible smells and head-splitting noise, were normal experiences shared by literally millions of men. What was not normal, at any rate in the memoirs, was finding oneself, on I September, 1914, having stated a false age in order to respond to Lord Kitchener's famous call to arms, grappling with the disciplines of a Reserve Cavalry Regiment (15th and 19th Hussars) and the requirements of some 2,000 horses. Parker reflects that it was probably the memory of the South African War that prompted the recruitment of large numbers of cavalry in 1914. He is clearly correct; the War Office would take a long time to shed the embarrassment of its response to the Dominion offers of help in that war against a totally mounted enemy only fourteen years earlier; the offers were accepted by telegram with the proviso, 'Dismounted Troops Preferred'.

By 1915, with trench warfare firmly established from Switzerland to the sea, the mistake was evident, and the pools of still untrained cavalrymen were switched to the hard-pressed infantry. Parker now found himself drafted to the Durham Light Infantry, a doughty regiment which raised no fewer than 37 battalions during the War, his being the 10th. The 10/DLI formed part of the 43rd Brigade in the 14th Division; this formation completed the 6-division tally of the 'first New Army' and, its infantry being composed entirely of Rifle or Light Infantry battalions, it was designated the 'Light Division', evoking thoughts of Wellington's Peninsular Army and the army of the Crimea. The famous regiments to which they all belonged had no difficulty in recruiting, some of the rifle battalions actually mustering 2,500 men apiece by the end of August, 1914.

Accordingly, on 11 September, the 14th Division's 'gigantic battalions' were paraded and split in half to form the second 'Light Division', the 20th, in the 'Second New Army'. But Parker and the 10/DLI remained in the 'First' Army, in the 14th Division.

The Division crossed to France on May 18, 1915, Parker following it in August in a reinforcement draft for the 10/DLI. They joined the battalion to the accompaniment of rumours of the 'diabolical effectiveness' of the German flame-throwers, which had just made their debut on the 14th Division sector at Ypres, an early novelty, presaging further nastiness in store. In 1916 the 10/DLI made acquaintance with the Somme, at Delville Wood, which was full of nastiness, and they had the satisfaction of clearing the Germans out of it (at a cost of 6 officers and 203 other ranks), only to learn two days later that the enemy had retaken the Wood in a massive counter-attack, always the feature of German tactics in 1916.

Parker met an attempt at this on 16 September at Gueudecourt, an action described in the chapter headed – with typical BEF irony – 'The First Tank Battle in World History'. Need I say that neither he nor his battalion caught sight of a tank that day? It was a bad time for the Durhams, caught by machine-gun fire from front and flank. Parker and one comrade found themselves in a crater, from which they observed a whole company of German Jagers rushing forward on their right:

> 'I kicked Stone and began firing rapidly over the top of the crater. By the time he had joined me, the dark green figures were drawing level with our position and now they began to falter, falling fast under our enfilading fire … we kept up the fire until all movement ceased and our ammunition was exhausted. When we looked at the bottom of the shell hole, there were two or three hundred empty cartridge cases under our feet … we began to realize that we had wiped out the whole company. It seemed strange that no one on the British side had joined in. Clearly we were alone.'

That was only a sample of the 'grit' which made it possible to endure the Somme battle and win it. The two Durhams remained in their crater under heavy artillery fire. When night fell they shifted back to a 'better 'ole', and began to dig in:

> 'Our new position overlooked the front on three sides, and presently we were joined by two or three other survivors who began to help us in digging our strong-point. We next collected ammunition, bombs, rations and food from the dead bodies which lay in long lines across the crest of the ridge … Our little band seemed to be the sole survivors of the Battalion … at the apex of a salient, marking the highest point reached by the attack. Not one of us thought of going back. On the contrary, we prepared to give the counter-attack of tomorrow a rough time.'

Kitchener's Army at its best.

For this and all else Parker was promoted to Corporal (acting Sergeant for a short time) and then applied for a commission. Just before Christmas, 1916, he and some more NCOs set off for England to join the Officer Cadet Battalion at Kimnel Camp near Rhyl, and his thoughts on the way there help us to understand what it was that made that little band of Durhams, apparently without any officers, commissioned or otherwise, decide to stay and give the inevitable German counter-attack a rough time at Gueudecourt:

'We caught through carriage windows fleeting glimpses of fields, peculiarly English in their neat hedge set patterns, of parish spires, screened by wintry trees, rising above the brown roofs of the cluster of cottages and securely tucked away in the peace of England's countryside ... these sweeping landscapes, devoid of traces of war's devilry, gave us a queer feeling of ownership ... At least in that hour, our recent adventures seemed worth while and death itself, now immeasurably distant, a fair price to pay for England's immunity.'

Parker's batch of cadets, he tells us, 'were keen, serious students of the art of war and they were trained by first-rate instructors.... When they finally returned to the battle fronts they brought an entirely new spirit into the ranks of the junior officers.' He had evidence of this in his new posting: the 2/Royal Fusiliers in the 29th Division, a Regular formation of Gallipoli fame and high reputation for efficiency on the Western Front. His own experience amply confirmed this, but he was not to be with the 29th for long; at Poelcappelle on 9 October, in one of the last sub-battles of what has gone down in history and legend as 'Passchendaele', and sharing almost the only self-evident success of that day (the division took 500 prisoners and 30 machine guns), he was wounded for the second time and he never returned to the front. He thus missed Cambrai and the return to open warfare in 1918, which from our point of view was just as well, since otherwise he would probably have been one of the 800,000 British casualties of that year, and we should never have received this minor classic.

John Terraine

E. W. Parker

Ernest Parker was born in Battersea during the closing years of Queen Victoria's reign – in fact just before her Diamond Jubilee. The house had been the marriage gift of his maternal grandfather, much of whose sagacity and determination Ernest inherited. His maternal grandfather was born in 1812, the year of the Retreat from Moscow, and died in 1911. Ernest was a late arrival much spoiled by three older sisters, the marriage of one of whom he attended at the age of six, armed with a pair of binoculars. That sister received two telegrams from the Queen on her sixtieth and seventieth wedding anniversaries.

The years before the First World War were not easy for the family; the building trade (his father was a builder) was very uncertain and Ernest, upset by constant rows over money, left school at fourteen to help.

By chance he found himself at Longmans Green and Co where Kelk, the office manager, spotted his talent and described him as the 'sea green incorruptible'.

Then, in the long hot summer of 1914, war was declared on 4 August and at once Ernest enlisted, before his eighteenth birthday on 13 September. His children loved to hear his tales of action and were very proud of the medals he won. After the war Ernest was determined to rejoin Longmans but it wasn't that easy. A young war hero can seem a little difficult to place in civilian life.

George Longman tried to persuade him that he was too good for the firm. Ernest countered by taking a wage cut. Soon, however, the firm appreciated him once more. Charles Longman described him as having a genius for the business and packed him off to America with a handsome new winter coat.

Ernest liked New York and Canada and wondered if he could introduce the habit of eating ice cream in winter to Britain! On his return to London he travelled for the firm, building up a knowledge of the trade. Then he was recalled to the office and was prolific in the list he built up. His colleague C. S. S. Higham sold the books all over the world and Ernest commissioned them. Between them they were the saving of the firm which had been in dire straits, rescued by an injection of cash from K. B. Potter.

On the advent of war in 1939 Ernest had been promised a part in a profit-sharing scheme, but was in no doubt where his duty lay. He despatched his family to Canada and joined up. He nearly found himself in the D-Day landing, but his age saved him at the last minute!

On his return to the firm he was sharply told to forget the profit-sharing scheme, so he bought a generous tranche of shares. This was, in the end, to be the making of him! Meanwhile he went on commissioning one successful book after another and by the late 1950s Longmans and Ernest Parker had become rich. He retired gracefully in 1963 as individually the most successful educational publisher in London and spent his remaining years playing golf with such dexterity as the Kaiser's bullets had left to him.

Into Battle 1914–1918

Into Battle

The naked earth is warm with spring,
And with green grass and bursting trees
Leans to the sun's gaze glorying,
And quivers in the sunny breeze;
And Life is colour and warmth and light,
And a striving evermore for these;
And he is dead who will not fight;
And who dies fighting has increase.

Julian Grenfell

Chapter 1

I Join the 15th Hussars

On the night of I September 1914, when I enlisted in Kitchener's Army, the War of 1914-18 was barely a month old and my eighteenth birthday was just approaching. I was far from being the youngest recruit, for in the queue was a boy of fifteen who lost his life on the Somme a couple of years later.

It took several hours before my turn came round and then I had to line up again to give my age as nineteen before I was finally accepted and given the order to report at the barracks on the following morning. For a couple of weeks I had been thinking seriously of joining up, and one by one my friends had already enlisted by the time I had decided where I thought my duty lay. All those young men were conscious of the threat to their country from the might of the Kaiser's Germany with its millions of well-trained conscripts, and it was general knowledge that our own small regular army, together with the territorials, would need every man who could bear arms if Britain was to survive. So although the army life did not appeal to me I took the plunge at last.

I was now a man under orders. The irrevocable step had been taken and, after getting my papers signed at the barracks, I dismissed my forebodings and set off for Bristol with a strange feeling of elation. I was doing the right thing and everything would turn out well – that reflection was to be my standby for the next four years.

When I was seated in the Bristol train at Paddington my fellow passenger, a middle-aged man, got into conversation with me and soon discovered my mission. He said cheerfully, 'The Army makes or mars', and left me wondering which my own fate would be. Luckily by the time I had passed through the gates of the cavalry barracks at Horfield I had forgotten my travelling companion's words or I should have imagined that I had already discovered which way the army would affect me.

That night when I wrapped myself in a brown blanket and stretched my limbs on the dew-saturated grass my worst fears seemed about to be realized. All around were thousands of recruits, yarning and making jokes into the early hours of the morning. Beneath the bright September stars I tossed restlessly from side to side to ease my projecting hips which pressed into the stones embedded in the grass. Far into the night the babel of voices rose and fell while I listened to the strange tales and queer outlandish speech of men drawn from all parts of the British Isles.

With the dawn the most restless threw off their blankets and began to look for water. When we discovered a tap we had to queue up to share the one piece of soap we could muster between us, and long before I was drying my face with a pocket handkerchief the whole camp was astir and men were walking up and down to get the circulation back to stiffened limbs.

Soon there were signs that our usual breakfast-time had arrived. Sharp eyes kept scanning the door of the cookhouse and when hours later a line of buckets glinted in that direction everyone was afoot and each orderly was surrounded by a struggling mob of untidy, unshaven men. I didn't have a chance in that scramble and, more or less a spectator, I watched the lucky owners of mess tins making for safety out of the crowd. More often than not they lost the contents of their tins on the way! When the bread ration followed, that, too, went to the strong, some of whom found it possible to get two or more shares which they wolfed ravenously. When breakfast was over there was nothing to do but walk about. Fortunately I soon discovered a canteen and there I tasted food for the first time since leaving home.

In the afternoon we fell in on parade and afterwards, in some semblance of military formation, marched through the gates of the barracks into the streets of Bristol, there forming a long column of fours that presently wound its way across the open fields of the Downs.

Here we halted to suffer the boredom of idling while thousands of names were called over. At long last the monotonous, droning voice fell silent and we went swinging along to the railway station to begin a night journey in a direction unknown to any of us. Towards midnight our railway carriages were exchanged for small open trucks in which we were jolted slowly through a beautiful, but unfamiliar, countryside where from the spikes of the fir trees glittering dewpoints reflected the brilliance of the September stars. Feeling bitterly cold, but buoyed up with the spirit of adventure, we laughed heartily when the inevitable wag announced that 'they were sending us to Siberia', for it seemed literally true.

Nobody could guess where the journey would end and when at three o'clock in the morning we arrived at Long-moor in Hampshire all that could be seen were the roofs of a few army huts emerging bleakly above the sea of thick white mist. These huts were not for us; instead we were offered the open fields and one blanket apiece in which to curl up with the damp grass moistening our cheeks.

With the rise of the sun we gladly gave up the vain pursuit of sleep to meditate anxiously on the prospect of rations. With determination born of hunger, I waited in the crowd surrounding one of the tea buckets until the supply was exhausted. Then, like many more of my new comrades, I realized that I must go without.

As the sun mounted higher on this beautiful September morning the lack of food and sleep had its effect so that I felt faint and wondered bitterly if I should ever adjust myself to my new life. We spent the early morning in idleness looking on while a party of men under a sergeant began erecting bell tents. After we had watched with growing interest our turn came to take part in the work, and by the time the guy ropes of our own tent had been tightened, hundreds of white cones had sprung up, surrounding us with a still rapidly growing canvas town. Each tent in this encampment was to be the home of twenty men for the next month or so.

It would have been difficult even in Kitchener's Army to have found a tougher crowd than the owners of the forty feet that at sundown kicked their way towards the pole in the centre of our tent. Frequently during the night the tent flap was raised so that my head could be poked underneath to breathe the pure night air outside!

During the whole of September rations were of the scantiest. Tea buckets lacked milk and sugar, and though the bread ration came regularly we had to eat it without butter. At breakfast-time minute scraps of fat ham rewarded us on our return from early-morning stables. At last when a crowd assembled outside the Quartermaster's Stores several officers hurried to the spot to listen tactfully to a long string of grievances which they immediately promised to put right. From that day onwards there was a general improvement in the rations. What had happened to our food during the previous month is a mystery which has never been solved.

After living in the overcrowded tent for nearly two months, our little community of twenty men had learnt to live together in mutual friendliness in a way that would have seemed impossible at first. I was the butt of a group of Eastenders and I had to stand up for myself. Although no boxer, I managed to come off fairly satisfactorily when attacked.

Now with Winter in sight we moved into the mounted infantry huts which had been erected in the Boer War. In these comfortable quarters, with their pervasive odour of paraffin, I found myself among an entirely different group of men, more miscellaneous in calling and origin and much more pleasant as companions. One of them, however, was a peculiar character who suffered from incurable melancholy. One night when I had settled down in my bed he began muttering that he would have to end his life. This in itself was nothing new, but when I saw him draw out his razor I leapt out of bed, snatched it from him and flung it out of the window. On this the poor fellow accepted the position and weakly got into bed.

Another strange type was a young fellow from a reformatory who was constantly asking someone to punch him. That, of course, was something no one could do in cold blood, but if one clenched a fist, pretending to comply with this strange request, he would immediately fall down with a crash on the hard wooden floor and then get up smiling and happy at having shown off a trick he had learnt as part of his own special sort of education.

In my leisure time I tried to polish up my German, and when I heard of some evening French classes I turned up at the Army School where the band boys attended compulsorily. One evening only one of them was present and I learnt from him that all the rest had deserted. They were found a few weeks later working in the Bristol area. They were thrilled to think that in the outside world there was now a clamorous demand for the services of youngsters under military age.

Every evening while I was at Longmoor I paid a visit to the Soldiers' Home, where for fourpence, the price of twenty cigarettes, I could obtain a huge basin of porridge floating in milk. The old soldiers would have scorned such food, but for a teenager with a never-satisfied appetite this was just what was most needed after a hard day's work.

Cavalry life began at dawn, when we all turned out to parade for stables. Here we learnt the art of grooming restive horses, a task which helped us to anticipate the sort of difficulties we should meet when we had to ride them. It was several months before we could count on two rides a week; but in the meantime, when luck came our way, we went back to our less fortunate comrades with stories of quite unbroken remounts successfully gripped between our trembling knees.

Reports of this nature considerably increased my respect for the livelier animals in our collection, and when one morning it was my turn to take a particularly malicious black mare for squadron drill I was not at all enthusiastic, to say the least. My knees lacked grip, and until the black mare broke into a delicate, effortless trot I did not know what to expect. Then it seemed as if those dainty, spindle-like legs trod upon air instead of the much-trampled earth of the parade ground. Never before had riding been so comfortable, but I warily slackened the reins and remembered to keep my spurs clear of her sides as we cantered in fours on to the plain alongside the other troops of the squadron.

Advancing on the trumpet call 'Walk march!' we quickly broke into a trot, followed by a canter, with our drawn and pointed swords flashing in a long line across the plain. Sounding above the jingling of harness and the clattering rattle of our empty scabbards, we heard the thrilling notes of the call to charge. Away we went, steadily at first, each horse accelerating as its reserves of strength allowed. Soon I was abreast of our squadron commander whose furious red face, turning in my direction, was convulsed in anger. In a trice he was outpaced and left so far behind that his raucous voice could no longer be heard. Then, as happened on great occasions subsequently, my spirits rose and with my young heart galloping in time with the racing feet of my splendid mount, I found myself leading the charge.

Now 'Retreat' was sounded by the trumpeter, and at last the little black mare made terms, and we returned to overtake the squadron in full retreat. Rejoining its bunched ranks we were welcomed by viciously raised hooves, but despite such malice we squeezed through so violently that we arrived once more in a leading position on the other side.

At this point the little mare made a bid for freedom. In a sudden frenzy she reared up and toppled over sideways, pinning me to the ground. Luckily, before she could get up I seized the reins and so held her down long enough for two troopers to gallop up and save me from being dragged at her heels.

One fine Spring morning in 1915 we set off in pairs on a Point and Compass race. It was one of my lucky days, for beneath me cantered the same little black mare in a thoroughly good temper. Before long my companion was hopelessly outdistanced and, easing to a canter, we sped across the Hampshire Downs and saw scattered on the tops of the hills small round copses of trees standing out against the skyline, marking the buried bones of some bygone race of warriors, and helping a younger generation to find their way by map and compass.

Taking every jump that offered, I came at last to a country lane where I drew up to await my companion. When he overtook me I again forged ahead until confronted by a strong, five-barred gate. Intending to dismount, I took my right foot out of the stirrup and felt the plucky little mare brace her muscles to fly smoothly over the top-most bar. As she landed softly, I realized with surprise that I was still in the saddle.

When the routine of Longmoor Camp had at last been organized, the life led by the cavalry recruits grew more strenuous. At dawn we paraded for the stables 'to water your horses and give them some corn'. After breakfast we went riding and returned before lunch to groom and feed our chargers. About two o'clock everybody except the old soldiers turned out for foot drill, and on the parade ground small groups of men performed under their N.C.O.s an astonishing variety of exercises. One squad of men with drawn swords lunged with assumed ferocity towards a neighbouring group of men who marched and wheeled in a bewildering pattern of cavalry movements; others were mastering the mysteries of musketry or succumbing to the boredom of rifle drill; while in the distance we could have heard, had we kept silence for a few minutes, the powerful snoring in chorus of the 'old sweats' who had contemptuously turned into their bunks after midday dinner.

Occasionally this daily cycle of duties was interrupted when we were detailed for Guard Duty. On these occasions we 'rookies' were obliged to borrow the khaki uniform of an old soldier and then for twenty-four hours we could imagine that we were real soldiers. This gave us the thrill of adventure, and after undergoing the ordeal of inspection by the Adjutant we looked forward to our turn of sentry duty with the feelings of men about to fight their first battle. Apart from the prospect of catching a spy red-handed, which always seemed worth bearing in mind, we knew that inside the Guard Room, and entrusted to our sole care, were several desperadoes whose military crimes might be augmented at any moment by a desperate bid for freedom. It was well that inquisitive officers did not often test our vigilance, for with such possibilities in our minds we were ready to shoot at sight.

The Water Guard was not taken so seriously, although we were impressed by the fact that it was a rather vulnerable place, and that on any night an attempt to poison the whole camp might have to be frustrated by the determined use of our rifles. Half-way through the night our ardour usually cooled off, and now and then we stealthily puffed cigarettes while maintaining a sharp look-out for the approach of the visiting rounds.

The hours spent in this pleasant spot were not altogether wasted. We grew fond of the deep pool in which the surrounding hills, with their thickly wooded slopes, were reflected in crystal clear water. In April 1915 we began to swim there on the holiday afternoons when the old cavalrymen enjoyed their privilege of sleep.

About this time we discovered that over the hills a company of R.E.s were constructing a narrow-gauge railway. One evening when we visited the spot we found it deserted. The railway lines had been completed and lying on its side near by was a small flat-topped truck. This we lifted on to the rails and laboriously pushed to the crest of the hill where we loaded ourselves toboggan-fashion on to its flattop. Then off we started downhill, gathering speed until the air whistled through our ears, and the wheels tore along the tracks. By the time news of this discovery had spread throughout the camp there was a nasty accident, and a notice in Battalion Orders placed our switch-back railway out of bounds.

One day when the men of the 15th and 19th Hussars Cavalry Reserve Regiment were still wearing red tunics, blue trousers, khaki caps without badges, and the civilian boots in which they had enlisted, our acting Squadron Commander, Captain Dalgetty, paraded us to say that we were to hold ourselves in readiness to repel a threatened German attack at Scarborough, for the town had been bombarded from the sea. Although we ourselves heard no more of this false alarm, I learnt years later from one of the Lovat Scouts that they had been hurried to the threatened area and were, in fact, the cause of the delightful rumour that thousands of Russians were arriving in England with snow on their boots. A journalist, observing the queer outlandish uniform of the Scouts and their wild-looking mounts, asked one of my friend's comrades where they had come from. 'From Ross-shire', he said in broad Scots.

This was one of the few occasions when one of our officers bothered to speak to us. These cavalrymen were members of an exclusive military set and had their own ideas of discipline which, it must be admitted, worked extremely well. No doubt all their thoughts were on rejoining their units and getting back into action as quickly as possible, and probably if their subsequent careers could be traced it would be found that many achieved high command. Meanwhile they kept out of sight and left everything to a small band of N.C.O.s, dugouts like themselves, who treated us as they would have treated well-trained regular soldiers, many of whom did indeed leaven our ranks, bringing with them stories of the Boer War and of Omdurman.

Makeshift as everything was of necessity in an army swollen suddenly by the influx of thousands of untrained civilians, the system or lack of it worked amazingly well. There was little military crime; all duties were undertaken cheerfully and nobody complained. Yet for the first month we were half starved, and it was well into the New Year before we were equipped with khaki uniforms and stout army boots. Did the elegant dandies in the Officers' Mess ever discuss the quality of this huge mob of new recruits put into their charge? They certainly took no apparent pains to study the problem.

Just one attempt was made to brighten our winter in Longmoor. An enterprising subaltern with the distinguished name of Lieutenant The Maclaine of Lochbuie brought down a number of well-known actresses from the West End and organized a concert. This was a very popular event and, led by one of the actresses, we sang lustily the latest hits – 'Sister Susie' among them. That evening was remembered with gratitude by at least one of the two thousand cavalrymen whose subsequent paths no man will ever be able to trace.

When we were fighting the Boers at the turn of the century it was found necessary to raise a number of units of mounted infantry. No doubt it was the memory of this earlier war that led to the enlistment of so many cavalrymen in 1914. As soon as the first of the new service divisions found their way to the front, this pool of overlisted and not yet thoroughly trained cavalrymen was an obvious source of reinforcement, when, as happened so quickly, heavy casualties began to thin the ranks of the infantry battalions.

Chapter 2

Field Operations

I cannot distinctly remember the day when we first took part in field operations. For a long time rumour had been busy circulating the mysterious words throughout the camp, and we had spent many hours assembling war kit and fastening rolled greatcoats to our saddles. One morning the news was broken to us and after a hurried breakfast we mounted with difficulty over saddles loaded with active service kit. Quickly breaking into a trot, we rode off in fours to join the infantry of the Division near Borden. On approaching them we saw through the morning haze masses of marching men, winding in column on route through the furze-set heaths and disappearing in tiny spirals over the misty hill crests in the distance.

The formidable appearance of the infantry of the New Army surprised me, yet as the files of foot-sloggers passed by, backs bent beneath cumbersome packs and weighed down by the additional war equipment, a wave of genuine sympathy ran through our ranks. Following behind came a detachment of cyclists, and to cavalrymen there was something queerly amusing in watching their pedals rising and falling as we were carried jauntily past, chaffing them as we went.

One thing we shall not forget is the sight of thousands of rhythmically swinging kilts as a Division of Highlanders swept towards us. Skirling at the head of the column strode the pipers, filling the air with wild martial music. Behind glinted a forest of rifle barrels and the flash of brawny knees rising and straightening in rhythm. Were these the freemen of yesterday, peaceful citizens who a few months ago strolled to work? These men seemed to us a crack military unit ready to carry out its mission.

While we idly watched, the dwindling sound of the pipes was carried wailing into the distance, drawing the Highlanders towards their task, leaving us behind to consider mournfully our remote chance of active service. Just then the delay in starting our real task was the cause of much heartburning.

As the bright Spring days of 1915 passed by Kitchener's Army grew restless, while daily the infantry kept up their long route marches, expecting with every dawn that the day of departure had at last arrived. Rumours of the declining value of our own arm in the new conditions of warfare began to circulate, and when Divisions of the New Army embarked for France without a detachment of cavalry we became seriously alarmed. Why were we kept out of it? We had our answer promptly; on the Orderly Room notice board appeared an announcement that volunteers were wanted for the infantry. Very few failed to register their names, only to discover next morning that the authorities had been having a little joke, for regardless of the names of volunteers, lists were posted by installments drafting all of us to Northern infantry depots.

The final draft could at last satisfy their desire for horses. Before leaving we each took four animals for a gallop, thinking ourselves fortunate in returning with as many.

Chapter 3

Transferred to the Durham Light Infantry

After a fourteen-hour train journey we arrived at South Shields, having swallowed innumerable cups of tea and sticky buns on the way, for at all the main stations groups of ladies were waiting to offer refreshments to the troops in the passing trains. Now that red tunics and other odds and ends of clothing had been replaced by service khaki we felt less embarrassed in the presence of civilians. Indeed, during the distribution of such tokens of their patriotic appreciation we were constantly in danger of leaving behind some of our more gallant comrades.

Just why a condemned glass works had been chosen as our billet at South Shields those in authority knew best. We found it a filthy skeleton of a place with blackened and broken windows overlooking rearwards the dingy docks of the River Tyne. In front, sentries were posted with fixed bayonets, and one of their chief duties was the obstruction of the door to blowsy and hideous-looking women who apparently threatened the safety of the protected troops.

On the other hand, we had good luck in having an excellent officer, a Durham lieutenant, who at once won our confidence. Under his efficient supervision the improvised billet was cleaned and made habitable, and the carefully watched cookhouse began to provide excellent food, with the natural result that the cavalry draft turned into a contented body of men.

Two competent and friendly sergeants now took us in hand and in a few weeks we performed our drill like a smart infantry company. The annoying habit of numbering off in fours, instead of in the infantry way, began to wear off, and we even forgot to grouse about foot-slogging now that the time of our departure was approaching. Marching steadily to the light infantry quick step we cheerily roused the homes of this North Country town with many a lusty chorus from the London music halls.

All was not work at South Shields. Sometimes one or two of us would swim in the baths where we were startled by the black shell-shaped patches on the miners' bare backs. Once I persuaded three or four ex-cavalrymen to accompany me in a rowing boat in which we sallied forth into the North Sea, leaving the land a mile or so behind us. Suddenly I decided to have a swim and while I was enjoying myself in the water I noticed with some alarm that the boat was being rowed vigorously towards the mouth of the Tyne. Not being a strong swimmer I found myself left farther and farther behind, until at last my comrades in the boat got over their panic and came back to rescue me. Their alarm had been caused by a few porpoises disporting themselves in the distance, but these ex-Hussars had come from inland places and had never before seen the sea and its monsters!

Early in August we heard that we were considered ready for the front, but that no leave would be granted before embarkation. This came as a blow, yet only one man took French leave, and the rest of us hoped to see our families when the train passed through London. While crowds of relatives waited anxiously at the London terminus, however, we were shunted through the City's tunnels and departed without seeing them. The train thumped its way in secret to Folkestone, carrying us bitterly disappointed; yet relieved of the ordeal of parting.

One by one we tramped heavily up the gangway of the channel steamer to stow ourselves on the open decks, where we loosened our equipment and rested our heads on our bulging packs. Within arm's reach were laid our rifles, and overhead the stars shone through the gaps in the expanding clouds of smoke from the steamer's funnels. Across a motionless sea the troopship carved a firm white track. Drowsily breathing the salt-tanged air, we were lulled into quiet confidence in the success of our mission. After a few peaceful hours the engines were shut off and the boat glided noiselessly through the water and came into position by the quayside. At last the moment of destiny had arrived, and clumping awkwardly down the gangway the feet of its self-chosen liberators trod the soil of France.

> *Now, God be thanked Who has matched us with His hour,*
> *And caught our youth, and wakened us from sleeping,*
> *With hand made sure, clear eye, and sharpened power,*
> *To turn, as swimmers into cleanness leaping.*

Rupert Brooke

Chapter 4

The Durham Draft Lands in France

On landing at Boulogne we fell into the ranks and marched dreamily up a steep hill that to our sleep-drugged senses seemed never ending. At the first halt we sank backwards gratefully on to our packs, awakening a few minutes later from heavy slumber on the command 'Fall in'. In the rest camp of St. Martin's our broken slumbers were resumed for a few hours and then, after an early breakfast, we heard for the first time the gamins' monotonous petitions for 'Boolee bif' and 'Biskwi' as we marched to the station for Etaples.

The Base Camp of Etaples surprised us by its hordes of smart, teeth-snapping instructors who hungrily swooped down to hustle us through a lightning revision course of bayonet fighting, musketry, arms drill, and physical training. In addition to these familiar exercises we now learnt the use and adjustment of the new gauze-bandage type of gas mask which we tied round each other's mouths. Thus disguised we looked like a dentist's nightmare, and it was in no military spirit that we performed our rifle drill with these absurd rags checking our breathing.

While at the Base Camp we heard of an entirely new danger to be faced. The 10th Durhams, to whom we had been drafted, had just sustained a liquid fire attack at Hooge, and rumours of the diabolial effectiveness of the German *flammenwerfers* were circulated throughout the camp. Happily for us, these unpleasant tidings were forgotten when we eagerly began our journey up the line, filled with pleasure in leaving behind the myriads of sharp-eyed instructors whose farewells had made thousands of our predecessors similarly happy.

Hey nonny no!
Men are fools that wish to die!
Is't not fine to dance and sing
When the bells of death do ring?

Anonymous, Christ Church MS.

Chapter 5

The Journey up the Line

Our cattle truck, like its neighbours, was marked plainly *Hommes 40: Chevaux 8*, but a wonderful feat of compression squeezed fifty of us into it and it was with difficulty that we converted our packs into seats.

Before leaving the station the engine screamed in a bloodcurdling manner and began jerkily to tug the train forwards, jolting the trucks together with such violence that we were all piled into a heap on the floor. The engine, after this display of energy, now came to a standstill while the gamins in the roadway dolefully intoned 'Boolee bif – Biskwil' until we were irritated into audible protest. At this sign of recognition the plaintive wailings grew more insistent and to relieve our ears we aimed a fusillade of iron rations, reserved for emergencies, through the open doorway. We observed no casualties, however, and the successful little rascals gleefully wished us 'Bon Voyage!' as the train at last got under way. The snail's crawl of the engine had at least one advantage, for it allowed us to stretch our cramped limbs by walking alongside the cattle trucks. When this pastime grew boring we settled down like tourists to enjoy the scenery, noticing the toylike prettiness of the gaily painted villas, the solidly built chateaux with green shutters, surrounded by velvety paddocks and ancient gnarled trees. Occasionally we caught glimpses of jovial poilus waving to us from the village lanes, their gay reds and blues contrasting pleasantly with the golden thatch of the cottages. Everywhere we felt the quiet peace of the countryside where sun-saturated woodlands alternated with wide stretches of rich green pasture. These pictures of an unravaged France were photographed on our minds as we crept towards the desolation the memory of which they could surprisingly survive.

At the halting-places a few lucky people obtained hot water from the engine driver, while the rest of us looked on in envy as it was turned into strong dixie tea. Our prolonged singing of the 1915 repertoire had parched our throats so that we coveted that famous brew and collectively groaned when, in answer to our appeals, the last of the tea leaves were flung out across the metal rails. At Poperinghe we left the train at last and stretched our legs by marching along the cobbled Vlamertinghe road. Battered houses and broken-up shop fronts aroused our interest, and we estimated, rather wildly, the size of the shell that had crumpled the thick walls. Smashed bedsteads, mattress springs, splintered tables and bloodstained clothing had been gathered into untidy mounds in clearing the roadway, and the pathos of these relics stirred our indignation, for we looked at them on this first occasion with the eyes of civilians who had still to learn what war was like.

We now knew that at last we were about to enter into the Valley of the Shadow of Death. What effect this experience would have on our lives we could not imagine, but at least it was unlikely that we should survive without some sort of inner change. Towards this transmutation of our personalities we now marched.

> *They went with songs to the battle, they were young,*
> *Straight of limb, true of eye, steady and aglow.*
> *They were staunch to the end against odds uncounted,*
> *They fell with their faces to the foe.*

Laurence Binyon

Chapter 6

The Threshold

The transport camp of the 10th Durhams was in a field belonging to one of the outlying farms of Vlamertinghe. On our arrival here we fell out to put up small bivouacs roofed in with our groundsheets. Before turning in we went off in small groups to explore the neighbourhood, and soon made the discovery that the farm folk had been studying their new market problem, for they sold many useful articles to the troops.

Entering the farm kitchen, we sat down at a dirty table and ordered coffee and biscuits. The primitive bareness of the room, probably hundreds of years old, impressed us strangely, and through the smoke we watched the massive pot simmering over the fire, where it remained all day until the last embers had smouldered niggardly away. One result of this endless stewing was that with each cup the coffee grew in potency, and we had our money's worth, even though it was at the risk of being poisoned.

When we returned to the camp and had crept carefully into our tiny bivouacs, the heavy clouds broke and the sides of our flimsy shelters were lashed with violent rain. Through the earth beneath us streams of water came trickling and our clothes were quickly saturated. Gun flashes lit up the triangular ends of the bivouac, while the monotonous explosions gave us warning that our adventures were now close at hand.

Towards midnight we were turned out to go up the line. We set off in the gloom, and it was a comfort to us to feel the damp patches of our grey-backs gradually drying as our bodies became heated in marching along the Ypres-Vlamertinghe road. As we passed by that agonized

Belgian church, the sight of its leaning crucifix touched us poignantly, for it reminded us of the piety of its now dispossessed parishioners. This we contrasted with the nervous destructiveness of modern war, now revealing itself in the fitful light of a crescent of curling flames and the ominous dull booming of distant shelling.

After some miles of heavy marching in which the steady clop-clopping of high-lows wove itself into our unfinished dreams, we saw between the twin rows of staggering poplars a mass of battered towers and steeples thrusting skywards in black jagged outline against a background of fire and smoke. Before us stood the city of Ypres, grimly menacing our passage.

This was the solemn moment of our initiation when we began to examine our hearts to test their reaction to the cold stabbing fears these shadows of the future brought us. Death seemed to encompass us and its circling lights winked in warning while the night sky glared with menace. Now we drew closer to the queer wine-glass shaped water tower to make closer acquaintance with the crumpled suburbs of Ypres itself. Passing through the town, we came to the mounds of rubble on the flanks of the Cloth Hall, and as we noticed its remaining masses of heavy masonry, the wags were in great form – until, travelling rearwards from the guide, came the news that brought an awed silence. Underneath us lay deeply buried a complete company of the Cornwalls, recently entombed by a hurricane bombardment.

Through the gaping streets we followed the guide until at the Menin Gate we wheeled right and halted under the shelter of the ramparts. Here Regimental Sergeant-Major Noble turned out to welcome the new draft, and by means of a few staccato shouts divided us into four groups: each of which was allotted to a company. My chum joined 'B', while I turned to the left and became a unit in 'A'.

My new Company at once posted me to a dugout which I had to share with Ainslie, a short broad-shouldered miner, who led me to a small cavern by the Menin Gate and almost at the top of the rampart wall. Crawling through the entrance curtain, we felt our knees sink softly into a salvaged featherbed on which we slept soundly in spite of all the unfamiliar noises. When we awoke in the morning we learnt that such comfort must be purchased dearly and, itching all over, we discovered the strange bed-fellows who had evidently not wasted the night in slumber.

Putting our heads outside the dugout, we saw the whole Battalion astir and hard at it, chopping up wood with bayonets and jack knives to feed the flames of innumerable roaring fires. The pleasant smell of crackling wood mingling with the aroma of strong tea quickened our senses. In a few minutes we were watching our bright new dixies rapidly blackening over a blazing fire that devoured the fine splinters of wood as fast as knives could pare them off.

Around me was a sea of unfamiliar faces queerly different in type from any others I had known. Words like 'yam', 'cracket', 'ganin', reached me, and very little I heard could I understand. A queer army was Kitchener's.

Chapter 7

The First Working Party

At the close of that first day in Ypres we paraded for the nightly working party in no-man's land. With picks and shovels on our shoulders we passed through the Menin Gate and marched down the road as far as the West Lane communication trench. Here we got under cover, filing along until we came to the front line. On our way we were continually halting, now to wait until the rear got into touch; now to allow troops to pass us on their way back from the front line. Once or twice the words 'Way for stretcher-bearers!' rang out, and we held our breath while stalwart fellows carried past blanketed forms aloft on their stretchers. How soon would it be our turn? As we chaffed and told each other that we could do with a nice 'blighty', 'Wire high!' 'Mind your step!' and other messages came down the ranks from front to rear, teaching us the new march discipline of trench life.

We had already learnt much when we reached the front line, and now with great caution we crawled over the parapet and extended ourselves in the open to start work on a new trench. Officers warned us to stand still when the flares went up, and to our surprise we found that all the more experienced men froze still as statues as they were plainly silhouetted in the flare of the very-lights. Even when the machine-gunners got busy they remained perfectly motionless.

Until the trench grew deep we were not tempted to smoke, and talking was discouraged by our older comrades. When our shovels had carved their way down to water-level we felt safer, and began to exchange lights from cigarette-ends which we smoked in turns at the bottom of the deepening trench. We had now reached water-level, and my muscles ached as I heaved lumps of heavy liquid mud over the parapet. It was therefore a great relief when we were withdrawn into the communication trench to begin a sharp walk back to the ramparts. Although we returned without mishap, the people who had remained behind at Headquarters had been less fortunate. Most of the dugouts had been blown in by a heavy bombardment which had almost wiped out the H.Q. Staff. We were in consequence transferred to a trench outside the town, north of the Menin Road. Here we attempted to prepare some breakfast until alarmed officers rushed towards our smoke, threatening us with dreadful penalties. We therefore put out the fires, first dropping the tea into our dixies which were fortunately already boiling. All this seemed part of a great picnic to the men of the new draft accustomed to the communal cooking of army cooks.

After a few days we took over a trench in the support line behind 'C and 'D' Companies. The dugouts were tightly packed and into mine were squeezed four men, two at each end, which meant that I had on each side of my head two pairs of muddy boots. After spending some hours in this confined space it was a relief to step outside into the night air to prepare for a working party in the front line.

My memory of that first experience of the firing line is one of great tension. All the regular occupants seemed so desperately stealthy and noiseless. Alertness was written on every face, yet in spite of this awareness of the imminence of danger, when we visited the front line by day dixies of tea were boiling in every fire bay. As we passed by, stooping under heavy burdens, hot and panting in late August sunshine, although longing to share that tea we realized that the regular tenants needed it far more. The untried draft had great respect for the seasoned veterans in that as yet vaguely dreadful place. To us, in spite of their youth, they were experts in the craft of war.

Just when the first shell burst close at hand I cannot recall. Many times during the last few days we had ducked for shells exploding hundreds of yards away, and often we were scared by those screaming high overhead on their way to distant targets far to the rear. Possibly the first near bursts scared us less because there was a shorter interval of suspense, but when we were at last relieved and were marching down the Ypres–Vlamertinghe road, a shell actually struck the roadside within a yard or so of me. We remained tense until an older campaigner muttered the word 'dud'. This march was extremely painful, for on our arrival at Watou I found five punctures in my right heel, the result of projecting nails in one of my brand-new army boots.

In a field near Watou we erected a camp of bivouacs, and with the issue of blankets lived in comfortable quarters until the weather broke. In the meantime the men of the draft were constantly on parade for rifle drill, bayonet fighting and so on; for our new Battalion meant to show us its own superiority, indicating by these additional parades that we lacked the advantages of its original members.

After days like these, Carpenter and I enjoyed a quiet stroll to the village, where, escaping from serfdom, we could spend a peaceful evening in a cafe kept by Belgian refugees from Menin, who provided eggs and coffee for all comers. Pleasantly satisfied, we then returned across mangel-wurzle fields and over the bristling stalks of the reaped corn, enjoying a peaceful interlude in the golden light of a September evening, while we exchanged first impressions of trench life.

Next time 'A' Company was in the trenches it provided working parties in the firing line. On one of these nightly expeditions we had halted in the sunken road when I became conscious of a sickening smell that before long was to become familiar evidence of the unburied or disinterred dead. Strained voices from behind the groundsheet curtains of the dugouts kept warning us of the dangers of smoking. These regular inhabitants evidently suffered from nerves, and we were made to realize that we were, in fact, in the presence of the enemy, and that sometimes on these midnight pilgrimages the German trenches were perhaps only a score of yards away.

Here and there along the front line were snipers' posts, each with a small aperture which was closed with a steel shutter when not in use. One of the snipers let me fire a shot or two from his post, the quick reply warning us that this could be a perilous pastime, for the enemy's shots pinged against the shutter almost before we had time to close it.

At last our turn came for duty in the firing line, and there we found our duties allotted in a cycle of three hours, the first hour on sentry, the second sitting awake and alert beside the standing sentry, while the third was set aside for rest or miscellaneous duties. In my case the third hour was seldom spent in rest. Sometimes I was taken away to draw rations from the support line, and often I went out into the listening post, reached by crawling into a sap running out towards the German lines. I believe it is a fact that the section lance-corporal responsible for the distribution of duties was already out of his mind. During this wretched tour of duty he ate up most of the section's rations, and for the five days I was nearly starved and felt giddy for lack of sleep. This N.C.O. was reported missing when we left the front line and months afterwards he was arrested in the disguise of a Belgian peasant while engaged in the pleasant pastime of bombing the peasant's pigs.

At last the relief arrived and we were marching towards Ypres with Hell Fire Corner behind us. The machine-guns kept up their usual tap-tap-tap along the Menin Road, but even they could scarcely hurry us as we anxiously watched the Water Tower slowly creeping nearer. Now and then we dozed for a moment and missed the steady clop–clop of high-lows on the cobbles. Presently, looking in vain for the tower and realizing that it had been left behind, I discovered the possibility of sleeping on the march.

We began to suspect that our leader had lost his way. Bitter curses reached his ears and in obvious misery the subaltern tried to silence us. On and on we tramped without hope, and in the depressing fear that our weary steps would have to be retraced. At length we halted in a field and lay down on our greatcoats. Looking upwards at the stars sprinkling with silver dust a dark blue sky, I fell asleep.

Next morning we turned out at daybreak to complete the march to the Battalion Rest Camp which had eluded us overnight, and on our arrival we paraded for a visit to the Divisional Baths in Poperinghe. There, in batches of platoons, we handed in our clothing to the orderlies and took our turn in the tubs, kept warm by the continual addition of hot water. These improvised baths had been made by sawing in half the vats used for storing wine, and into each of them as many as four men would struggle with one piece of soap between them. After removing a month's dirt and thus thickening the water for our successors, we stood shivering while 'deloused' shirts and socks with our own fumigated tunics and slacks were handed over by the attendants.

Before long we discovered that deloused shirts were not what they claimed to be; for dormant under the seams at the arm pits were fresh platoons of the parasites ready to come to life as soon as they were taken under our protection.

In this way we maintained that the breeds were crossed, making them hardier and more pugnacious, so that they survived the ceaseless war we waged on them.

In the Winter we were robbed of pants, for after a week's wear they were overrun and had to be discarded.

Chapter 8

Our Part in the Battle of Loos

25 September 1915

It is better for us to perish in battle than to look
upon the outrage of our nation and our altars.

Ancient Church Service

Rumours of a big push had been reaching us for several weeks when, on 14 September, we arrived on the Menin Road by the White Chateau. In front of this unusually well-preserved landmark were the dugouts of the reserve line and these we occupied while the other brigades, together with our bombers, prepared for their attack on the following morning.

Strict orders forbade the lighting of fires, and these we completely ignored; guarding against the visits of outraged Authority, we pared off fine shavings of wood to boil by stealth the water for our tea. Overnight we made several journeys to the front line, taking up boxes of ammunition, afterwards returning to the dugouts, where we fell into a deep sleep.

At dawn the angry roar of the opening bombardment roused us, and for some time we lay speculating on our chances in our first battle. Presently a long, never-ending trickle of wounded men came filing back from the attacking waves. 'What is it like up there, chum?' we asked those bandaged, grey-faced men, and they told us after carrying the third line of trenches, the attack had completely failed; counter-attacking immediately, the Germans had regained all the ground we had won.

Following the attack, we moved forward into G.H.Q. line, noticing with horror some of our cavalry comrades whose dead bodies rested against the walls of the communication trench.

After vainly attempting to keep the rain out of our shelters all day, we returned at nightfall to the dump in the Menin Road, where each man collected picks, shovels, ammunition and rations. With these, and the inseparable burden of full marching order, we spent the night in misdirected wandering along a network of unfamiliar trenches behind the firing line. Balancing on one shoulder a box of ammunition, and, on the other, a rifle, I frequently slipped down into the mud, and during the short bursts of shelling I no longer cared to take cover, bitterly hoping to be blown to pieces and put out of my misery.

When we reached Muddy Lane (apt name) we were no longer goaded into fresh effort, and dropped thankfully into the damp earth to light our first cigarettes. Before the fag-ends were stamped into the mud, we were running up and down the crumbling trench as the enemy gunners bracketed the betrayed position. Utterly worn out, we gave up running and lay one on top of the other and so slept. When I awoke I heard that a man who had been resting his arms on my shoulders was now on the way to the Dressing Station with a wounded arm that probably saved me from a 'blighty'.

After 'stand to' the morning's rations were eaten, and we had begun to clean up the broken trench when it was discovered that the Battalion Aid Post was just behind us with our M.O. feverishly at work, his head swathed in a bloodstained bandage. Never before this moment had we realized his mettle. Later in the day, Comberland, the Battalion runner from over the border, stopped to tell us of his personal visit to Brother Fritz. After yesterday's luckless advance the cries of the marooned wounded tortured the ears of the front-line troops. In no-man's-land were scores of our own men whose pitiful appeals tore the hearts of their helpless comrades. At last, overcome by pity, Comberland sprang over the parapet and, waving his handkerchief, approached the German wire, where a tortured man was spreadeagled on the tenacious barbs. Below in the enemy trench an officer's head appeared, and with perfect sang-froid Comberland sprang sharply to attention and saluted, afterwards carrying back his wounded comrade.

Chapter 9

With the Transport and the Bombers

Soon after the Battle of Loos the remaining cavalry men were compulsorily transferred to the transport to fill up gaps made by recent casualties. At the Transport Camp we lived a peaceful life by day and enjoyed abundant rations skilfully prepared by our own cook. Grooming mules was often exciting. One of us at least never quite mastered the art of picking up their hind legs. When evening came we paraded with our mules, balancing two large panniers on each side of the pack saddles. With these ponderously swaying from side to side we journeyed in crocodile formation to the dump at the Dickebusch communication trench. Once we had unloaded the stores, pleasure began and seated astride the iron bars of the pack saddles, we cantered off merrily into safety. Thoughtfully our leader would halt us half-way, so that pipes could be loaded, and the mules rested. On one occasion the jolting of the beast's awkward trot flung my pipe on to the roadway. I managed to dismount a hundred yards further on, but the miserable animal refused to return. Listening with cocked ears to the rest of the troop clattering off down the cobbled road, he suddenly jerked me off my feet and in a mad gallop raced towards his brothers; when I at last scrambled over the iron bars I began to doubt my power over this sort of beast.

At the end of a fortnight the regular transport men began to return to duty and we in turn went back to our companies. At the time I entered the tent of my old section, emissaries from the bombers were busily searching for volunteers. During a recent spell in the trenches it had been noted that I lacked the proper respect for this new weapon. I had actually ignored a hanging bandolier of bombs which had served to screen my fire while I made tea. The excited bombing corporal who rescued it now claimed me as a proselyte, and I became a member of the toughest crowd in the Battalion. As a bomber life became one long escape from fatigues and rifle drill. While rifles were sloped, presented, ordered, ported, canted, trailed and bayoneted, we stole off to fill jam tins with mud in order to shy them at a target. Now and then fresh recruits were returned to duty when it was found that bad nerves made them fumble with lighted bombs. We got rid of them with relief, for they were unpleasant neighbours to have around. The rest of us formed a community within the Battalion and, supported by our own bombing N.C.O.s, stubbornly defied all attempts to make us work or drill. As a last resort, we had a pleasant trick of dropping bombs with feigned clumsiness which, with most of the uninitiated, achieved infallibly the result we wished.

Before the invention of the Mills bomb, the earlier experiments were distinctly dangerous. The Newton Pippin had to be struck against the end of the handle of an entrenching tool to ignite the fuse, while that of another grenade was fired by striking it on the side of a match box. We had good cause to remember these primitive weapons, for once, when the whole Battalion was halted in column of route in the narrow streets of Poperinghe, one of our comrades, Private Hoare, dropped all his Newton Pippins on to the cobbled roadway while stooping down to tighten his puttees. The consequent explosions just ahead of 'A' Company caused forty or fifty casualties in the crowded ranks. On another occasion the man in charge of the bomb store had a similar accident and heroically screened his comrades outside by taking the full blast of the explosion himself.

The next sector which it came to our turn to hold was St. Julien, farther to the left of the salient. Here we could walk about boldly after sundown in front of the trenches, and as bombers we patrolled no-man's-land all night with the Germans many hundreds of yards away. Winter was now upon us in earnest, and with the first fall of snow I took my share of the rum ration and felt it creeping slowly down to my frozen feet. It was a fatherly sergeant who persuaded me to sink my teetotal prejudices, and I still remember his sensible arguments.

We spent Christmas Day 1915 out of the line, and about this time we were turned out for inspection by General Sir Douglas Haig, who had then just taken over from Sir John French. His kindly eyes looked into mine as he passed along the ranks of the bombers, and he scarcely seemed to notice the antics of Blenkinsop, who, as right-hand man, had to fix his bayonet on a rifle cut down to less than half its original length. The rehearsal of this unmilitary manoeuvre appealed strongly to the Durhams' sense of humour, but much to our relief it all passed off without comment when the new G.O.C.'s inspection actually took place.

Another move leftwards put us in possession of the waterlogged trenches in front of Elverdinghe, and here in six-day reliefs we spent the remainder of the winter. Before our first march into the line, we changed into thigh boots, and by the time we reached it the ill-fitting boots (mine were size 10, but my feet were size 8) had nearly exhausted our strength. The bombers had to go further than their comrades, in order to occupy the outposts, isolated in front of the firing line. My section crept out gingerly over the treacly mud and, one by one, jumped across a trench which was falling in. Missing my footing, I dropped into an oozing quagmire of mud, and my comrades, slithering in the mud on top, had to lie down and attempt to tug me out. In doing so they pulled me clean out of my boots, themselves slipping backwards in a heap into the slime. All efforts to discover my boots failed, and the exertion left me helpless and at the end of my strength. Half carried, I returned to the main trench where, under some pieces of corrugated iron, I slept off my exhaustion, to find on waking the mud hard caked on to my clothes. The cause of my return to consciousness was the voice of Sergeant Goodge, who had discovered me during his inspection of the line. This good-hearted fellow took me to a fire and lent me his spare pair of riding breeches, afterwards preparing some hot tea.

Every time the Battalion went into the line at Elverdinghe the bombers held the outposts, and one night when I fetched the rum ration for the section, I returned by mistake with a dixie half full. Matty Parker and the other stalwarts were loud in their praises, but soon became incoherent, retiring heavily into the shelter to fall fast asleep.

Fortunately when Captain Pumphrey visited us I challenged him smartly, but to my horror I noticed too late that the other sentry was asleep. Corporal Matty Parker was severely reprimanded, but when we came out of the line no one was placed under arrest and we realized that our dear old Bombing Officer had not reported us. In consequence we were all thoroughly disgusted with ourselves.

It was at Elverdinghe that we were first equipped with shrapnel helmets, yet another addition to the enormous load we carried wherever we went.

Chapter 10

Good-bye to Ypres

Just before we left this sector the Germans opened up a stiff bombardment and tried to penetrate our lines. Several parties came close to the bombing posts, but the attacks withered away under our fire. Directly we were relieved, another German attack captured the front line from our successors.

We marched back through a snowstorm to Houtkerke, where circumstantial rumours of our transfer to Egypt became insistent. Instead, we were destined for the Arras front, as yet held by the French. After a train journey to Vignacourt, we began a four-day march on roads covered with frozen snow, and during this bitter weather the transports lagged behind, leaving us to manage with scanty iron rations. Before starting from Vignacourt, we queued up in vain before the local *boulangerie*, hungrily smelling the baking loaves which our money could not buy. Instead, we breakfasted on biscuits and began a fifteen-mile march to Beauval. On the third day I could not keep my balance, loaded as we all were with full marching order under our capes, and I counted thirteen falls on the treacherous road. As we entered Simencourt my comrades supported me, taking my rifle and half carrying me into the barn, where I fell down totally exhausted. Again Sergeant Goodge came to the rescue and took me into a café, where I began to pull round. On the following day I was left in a house with some French refugees who treated me most hospitably, and as a result of their excellent cooking I soon felt fit. I joined the Battalion next day by riding on a limber and we entered Achicourt to relieve the French, who were needed for the defence of Verdun. As they left they kept shouting joyfully: 'À Verdun! À Verdun!'

It was immediately after my recovery from that grueling march that Captain Pumphrey gave me my first lance stripe. He had noticed that I had stuck it out and said with his usual stutter just the right things to encourage a youngster like myself.

We observed with interest that our allies had been holding their line in a different way. Deep dugouts had been tunneled into the chalk; faggots were laid in readiness on the parapets in case of attack by gas; and the deep trenches were both floor-boarded and well revetted with fascines. Our greatest surprise was in the almost complete absence of shell or rifle fire, but quite as remarkable was the presence of civilians in the villages, less than a mile from the German front line. These hardy folk persisted in tilling their land while the long-range shells from both sides roared through the sky high above their heads.

Before leaving Elverdinghe I had allowed one of my gum boots to get scorched, with the consequence that a large burn appeared on my leg. This had been neglected and now developed as a running wound which had the effect of taking me daily out of the line for medical attention at Battalion H.Q. I used to enjoy the quiet walk along the deep communication trench into the battered village of Agny, where, with the approach of Spring, the flowers began to struggle through the ruins and to cover up the wounds of war.

One day a shell splinter wounded my neck, but it was dressed by stretcher-bearers and I did not report it.

Gradually the British tried to introduce a more offensive spirit into the war on this sector of the front. Sometimes we went out into no-man's-land and, approaching within the range of the German lines, fired off half a dozen Hales rifle grenades without being at all sure that they would arrive in the enemy's trench. Sniping, too, was developed, and from the point where our front line crossed the railway cutting, we occasionally picked off grey figures descending into the cutting in the enemy's trench. When bored by the lack of enemy movement we amused ourselves by shooting off the insulators on the telegraph poles, and one day the other people began the same stunt. We were startled to find that their marksmanship was first-rate, for each time a rifle was fired an insulator was smashed.

It was discovered that nearly all the bombers in 'A' Company were suffering from scabies, and without delay we were marched off to the hospital at Froment. Here we donned hospital blue and had great fun baiting the R.A.M.C. orderlies whose neatly oiled hair and smart mud-free uniforms had an irritating effect on our ruffianly crowd of Durham bombers. When the sleek-haired orderlies officiously mentioned that we were confined to camp, we cheered up and stealthily changed into khaki, climbed the fence and prepared to spend a hectic night in the village. So fearful were the R.A.M.C. orderlies that they forgot to report us. Next day with great relief we exchanged soldier's farewells when the M.O. found we were free from the suspected complaint.

One of the advantages my lance stripe conferred on me was the duty of orderly corporal. When the weather improved I took advantage of my visits to Battalion H.Q. to swim in a pool near an old mill. Although it was within a mile of the enemy, the surroundings were as peaceful as any rural scene in England. There were other pleasant features of this restful period, and without permission we walked into Arras to buy cigarettes, condensed milk, etc., at the canteen. On the way we used to climb through the ruins of a former candle factory, where huge barrels sprawled untidily around the wreckage of rusted machinery, and candle grease oozed in miniature glaciers among the piles of broken bricks.

Before leaving this sector we witnessed a big flare-up on the left of our front. Vimy Ridge was being attacked, and from our safe trenches we watched the shells lighting up the night. When next evening the flaming crescent of bursting shells had bitten further into the enemy's line all my tough comrades wished that they were there.

Army food was monotonous and in the line bully beef and bread, often without butter or jam, was the usual fare. Teenagers like myself were always hungry, and once we were back in rest billets we supplemented our rations with eggs if we had any money left from our pay, usually five francs, to buy such extras. Alas, when we needed food most it sometimes did not arrive at all, and it was far from pleasant to spend twenty-four hours or more in the front line without anything whatever to eat. Sometimes when drinking water did not arrive we were driven to boiling rain water from shell holes, and this may account for the crop of boils and diarrhoea that plagued us throughout the winter of 1915-16.

The chief reason for the non-arrival of rations was, of course, the enemy's shelling of our communications, but I shrewdly suspect that at all stages from the base to the front line vast quantities of goods were diverted to those more favourably placed. Even the N.C.O.s held on to the tin of butter intended for division among the platoon, while H.Q. Officers' Messes in the rear wallowed in a superabundance of good food of all kinds. No wonder the front-line soldier was always hungry.

Chapter 11

Tunnelling and Patrolling

The day came when we turned our backs on Agny for the last time, leaving behind one of the safest trench systems we had known. For 'A' Company the immediate prospect was not disagreeable, and we settled down in great comfort on the floors of a Convent School for the Blind in the heart of the City of Arras. In spite of its many battered buildings, Arras then had a peaceful atmosphere that cheered our spirits after so many months of trench dugouts. By night the shops in the main street lit their lamps, and fascinated our eyes with their display of peace-time goods. We liked walking through that street even though our pockets were empty, for the sight of the glittering windows transported us in thought to our own home towns, already a blurred, half-forgotten memory. Towards evening we daily journeyed to the front line and there, in shifts of eight hours, worked under the orders of a company of New Zealand sappers who were tunnelling under the German trenches. At the top of the sap, we hauled a continuous stream of chalk-filled sandbags, carrying them outside and unloading the chalk some distance from the sap head. By special favour, I was sometimes allowed to crawl down the deep shaft, where I could watch the tall New Zealanders cautiously working at the rock face. Now and then we listened in, and heard the enemy working in their counter saps.

Naturally our Durham miners enjoyed this heavy work immensely. They could imagine they were home again, and by comparison the present task seemed absurdly light. I found it hard-going enough during the eight hours when, without a break, we hoisted the sand bags of chalk on to our shoulders and staggered under them to the dump, twenty yards down the trench. But when five o'clock in the morning came, and we filed into the communication trench, sleepily finding our way back to the point where we could get out into the open, we all felt happy. With the sun growing warmer, we spread out across the fields and hungrily picked raspberries, red currants and strawberries, now growing wild in the deserted market gardens. Taking our time, we returned to the billet where a tea and bacon breakfast was ready on our arrival and then, already half asleep, we dropped heavily on to the wooden floor and slept soundly until the orderly men shouted 'Dinner up!'

Towards the end of June 1916 we moved into another Arras sector. While we were enjoying a quiet time in the support line, the platoon commander began to rely on me as a companion for nightly patrols in no–man's–land. We knew that the Germans were well entrenched behind several thick lines of wire entanglements, and it was generally fairly safe to go across to the first line of wire spending an hour or so, listening to the voices in the trenches, and the tapping sounds made by working parties. Occasionally we noticed figures moving against the skyline and then we waited for some time before going forward.

One day Lieutenant Marks told me that the Battalion must take a German prisoner, and I arranged to pick six men who would be willing to raid the German trench. That night we crawled up to the enemy's wire, and after an interval, I began to clip the first strands. After successfully cutting two or three without arousing attention, the next strand sprang apart with a fearful clatter and the alarmed Germans immediately took notice, opening up a rapid fire over our heads. Excited guttural conversation went on for some time and we heard with alarming distinctness the footsteps of the N.C.O. marching along the duck boards to a post on our right. 'Schiessen!' and another group of rifles came into action, their bullets whipping through the grass, uncomfortably close to our heads. Then the footsteps returned and travelled over the left where a third post opened up. After this, we heard a rustling noise in the grass and had the unpleasant feeling that a dog was nosing his way towards us. It came nearer and nearer and then, to our relief, returned into the trench. Meanwhile we all shammed dead; lying with faces buried in the grass, scarcely daring to breathe. After waiting with hair on end and expecting discovery, I must have relaxed and have fallen asleep. Several hours later, one of my comrades aroused me and then in single file we crept silently back to our own line. Just as we climbed over the parapet, the pale light of dawn appeared above the trenches opposite, and now, safely in our own trench, we all laughed heartily at the night's adventure, especially at the scare I had given Lazenby when he found that he had to wake me noiselessly under the noses of the Germans.

> *There was a time when meadow, grove and stream,*
> *The earth, and every common sight,*
> > *To me did seem*
> > *Apparelled in celestial light,*
> *The glory and the freshness of a dream.*
> *It is not now as it has been of yore; –*
> > *Turn wheresoever I may,*
> > *By night or day,*
> *The things which I have seen I now can see no more.*

Wordsworth

Chapter 12

The Anvil: Our Introduction to the Somme

A night came when we were relieved and marched into the outskirts of Arras to wait incredulously for the mythical buses. I was so heavy with sleep that as soon as my body touched the cobbled road I lost consciousness, and when the troops boarded the buses I was the last to climb up the steps. Selecting the gangway on top, I stretched out full length and slept soundly until aroused by our arrival at Avesnes-le-Comte.

News from the Somme had already reached us when we began a series of long route marches across the pleasant countryside of France. In that hot July weather, with sweat running down in thick drops from our faces, we laboured slowly along roads stirred into heavy breath-choking dust as the pageant of the Armies of the Empire paraded for the South. Swaying rhythmically in their saddles came the swarthy troops of Indian cavalrymen who with solemn dignity gazed down on our toiling spirals of infantry lining the right-hand side of the roadway. As we looked up at their fierce turbanned faces and long beards, and glanced at the glittering lance points, we felt the thrill of the approaching battle, and unconsciously lengthened our stride until checked by angry protests from the rear.

After the first day's broiling July sunshine some of the more reckless turned their slacks into shorts, and put into their packs the sleeves of their greybacks. In this greater freedom we overtook the remnant of the Guards, whose build seemed to render them less capable of staying the course in this sultry weather.

Passing from time to time under the shady arches of the tall poplars, beautiful as a cathedral nave, we wound our way past orchards drooping with ripening fruit, cottages speaking comfort and sweet peace, inviting us to stay and billet. Still on, climbing undulating roads, bare of habitation, fields of corn waving in the breeze to the horizon's edge, no landmark creeping slowly towards us. Now with eyes turned earthwards we plodded on uphill. 'How far is it now?' 'Only another kilometre.' It had been another kilometre for the last ten miles, and we forgot all else in striving to reach the top of the hill. Jerking pack straps to another part of our aching shoulders, we began to climb the easier slope of the rounded crest. At last when we dared to raise our eyes, refusing to hope, a reassuring vision of comfort spread before us. Below in the valley lay a pretty village, half buried in the protecting foliage of a thousand trees, with a graceful spire tapering high over all.

Descending into this snug, old-world hamlet, we were split up among its scattered houses and barns. Imagine the surprise of 'A' Company's bombers when it was discovered that inside their barn still remained an enormous barrel of cider! Round the barn hung great clusters of reddening apples, while the next building in the village displayed an ancient rusty sign inviting us to sample the beverages of France.

In these idyllic surroundings we were happy. Golden fields rippling in the wind healed the sight of our eyes, and the green depths of the woodland shadows, like soft music, quietened the tortured nerves of our bodies. We awoke in our barns at sunrise to hear, not the angry crashes of the morning strafe, but the forgotten songs of birds.

After some days of marching we knew by signs that we were approaching 'the anvil'. Already weary battalions of the strength of companies were passing us on their return from the battle area, and the men in their ranks bore on their faces the marks of strain and the tension of fighting. Division after returning division marched by, furnishing grim evidence of the toll of the Somme.

With Albert and its horizontal Virgin etching itself as an unforgettable picture before us, we halted, and on a hillside made a camp of bivouacs. Then by platoons we went down the valley and prepared to swim in a rippling and shallow stream of clear, swift-flowing water through which we could see the sharp flints soon to leave long scratches on our knees.

Sunbathing on the banks of the stream, we watched our gallant array of observation balloons floating lazily overhead; then, as we idly gazed, we heard the droning of a distant aeroplane high above the clouds. Swift as thought, a Taube dived through its screen of clouds and, as we waited tensely, swooped downwards to the nearest sausage balloon, rattling its machine-gun. Then it turned gracefully upwards as the glittering fabric of its victim shrank and burst into a glorious ball of fire and smoke. Long before the popping Archies began to fill the sky with woolly grey puffs of smoke, the daring pilot was again safely under cover behind the clouds. Soon another, and then another of our artillery's eyes flamed into the sky, while suspended in the air beneath these gigantic fireworks were the slowly descending parachutes of the swinging observers.

Next day we saw the remains of Fricourt and, passing through Montauban, picked up our guides at Pommier's Redoubt. Then leaving High Wood to the right, we entered a communication trench, and learnt that our destination was Delville Wood. At Longueval we came out into the open and found the crumpled bricks of a shattered village, still littered with bodies long dead. The village pond, once green, was now a vivid red and the corpses we stepped over were mainly those of the South Africans whose faces were blackened by three weeks of hot sunshine. At the edge of the wood we came into full view of the watchful enemy and therefore advanced by short rushes, each of which drew a long burst of machine-gun fire, and the soon-to-be-dreaded point-blank stab of screaming whizz-bangs. One section remained motionless in line sprawled on the ground never to move again, and in my mind's eye one man, Allen, is kneeling still where the gunners caught him preparing for the forward rush. We who escaped that murderous fire thankfully took cover in the trench, and relieved the Buffs whose retreat we followed by means of the repeated crackling of rifle fire that pursued them out of that accursed wood.

The trenches we now held were far too shallow, but any attempt to deepen them was purchased by immediate casualties, for the Bosch had but to aim his whizz-bangs at the tree stumps behind to fill our trench with flying shrapnel. In this way our platoon sergeant received a piece of metal through the stomach, and as we vainly attempted to push back his entrails he died in our arms. Soon afterwards we lost our heftiest bomber with what we more than suspected was a self-inflicted wound, this being the second case in my experience of France.

On the second day we were helping to bring up the rations from the support to the front line when the whizz-bangs caught us in the shallow communication trench. The first burst killed two men and the rest had to jump over their earth-covered bodies as the German gunners, in bracketing, made us run first up, and then down, the trench. Several people had trampled on them already and in getting across that dreadful mound of reddening earth, it was hard to avoid the soft springy place beneath which our comrades were so freshly buried.

That night three bombing corporals arranged to go out on patrol. We walked into the front line and first visited the latrine, where a man's booted leg projecting from the bench served as a hanger for our equipment. No-man's-land in the wood was a complete surprise. After the incessant strafing of the trenches, here was a sanctuary of quiet, filled with the dense blackness of the deep shell holes and uncanny shapes of the tortured trees. At every step we paused, listening intently, for with so much cover, surprise would be easy. Presently we gained confidence through our familiarity with the darkness, yet we were so near the enemy trench that it was wise not to venture too far, and after a couple of hours of peace we returned to our own trench.

After we had had one or two periods in the line at Delville Wood, we marched out to Bray for a rest. All the way out I limped badly, and discovered when I removed my boots a big swelling, like a boil, on my right heel. Next morning I reported sick and was packed off to hospital with a septic foot. The two stretcher-bearers who wheeled me out of camp pretended to be disgusted at having to push an able-bodied man after handling so many severely injured cases; but the good fellows were only congratulating me in the usual way, and in parting they wished me many days of hospital. In two or three days I was fit and returned to the transport camp in Happy Valley. On my arrival with a batch of men similarly reporting for duty, I was told to wait for the Battalion, and in the evening my comrades came back, their eyes shining, from a successful bombing attack. They had cleared the last German trench in Delville Wood, and were returning with its total removable contents, judging by the numbers of field glasses, automatic revolvers, cigars, and strange tins of mixed butter and jam they carried. Their most curious discovery was that, instead of drinking chlorinated water like us, the Germans were supplied with mineral water manufactured in one of the French villages behind the line.

Feeling that I had missed the best show yet, I marched sadly back to Corbie.

It was on 8 August 1916 that our battalion had arrived at Happy Valley and our first spell in Delville Wood began five days later. When after a brief rest the 10th Durhams returned there they found that Edge Trench, on the northern verge of the wood, was still partly in the hands of the enemy. It was my own comrades in the bombers who bore the brunt of clearing them out, for they not only seized Edge Trench but pushed along the old German communication trenches. It was in this action that we first came up against the German stick-grenades, a weapon which struck us as being more effective than our own Mills bombs. We called them potato mashers which they resembled in appearance. All this was at a heavy cost of no less than six officers and 203 men, among them our much-beloved bombing officer, Captain Pumphrey, who lost a leg.

> *Whither shall I go then from thy spirit,*
> *or whither shall I flee then from thy face?*
> *If I climb up into heaven, Thou art there:*
> *If I lay me down in hell, Thou art there also.*

Psalm 139 modified by Robert Bridges

Chapter 13

The First Tank Battle in World History

Our billets after this show were the most comfortable we had ever had. So far the village had been unspoiled, and consequently we found the French people very pleasant and friendly. The first night was a wild one, for the captured automatic revolvers and field glasses found plenty of purchasers, and wine flowed as never before in the quiet old village *estaminets*, now filled with Durhams. Far into the night revolver shots were fired at the moon, and before morning not only the Guard Room, but the field used as an annexe, was overflowing. So many cases called for summary treatment, but as we were due for another attack and needed training, only the worst cases received field punishment and the rest worked off by long runs in extended order the previous evening's dissipation.

Again we camped on the hillside by Albert. Presently an angry voice stirred the troops, and we hastily fell in to be soundly abused for allowing our hair to grow long. Major S – had come back to take charge of the Battalion after a long period of duty as Town Major, or some similar rest cure. Hearing we had no battalion barbers, he sent for clippers from the transport camp, making us form long queues to await our turn for 'shaving'. So coarse were the clippers that many heads were bleeding after the operation. Our sergeant, Matty Parker, a very good-looking young fellow, was nearly due for leave and the operation left him so disgusted that he actually shaved a crescent of hair from his forehead and with an indelible pencil inscribed thereon his name, rank and regimental number. Next time he went up the line a bullet removed just that portion of his face.

Major S – , following his usual habit, returned to his safe job and when Colonel Morant took over he assembled the Battalion and explained our next attack. We then heard of a new weapon, 'the tank', which it was hoped would take the enemy completely by surprise, so that at last the cavalry would break through and finish the war.

On the now familiar road to Montauban we passed stray troops of cavalry and we felt that something out of the ordinary was happening, but for all our curiosity to examine the new tanks not one was to be seen and most of us went through the attack without that experience. At Pommiers Redoubt we found dugouts, but we at once paraded for a carrying party to the Wood. Each of us struggled with six Stokes mortar bombs and the work took ten hours. Before we had time to eat, we were again turned out, this time carrying 'toffee apples' – mortar shells weighing about 60 lb. So unlucky was I that when I staggered back to the dugouts, reeling with fatigue, the Orderly Sergeant shouted to me to fall in for a third carrying party, and now a fresh officer bullied us to keep up our pace until we were at the end of our strength. Arrived at last in a dugout back in Pommiers Redoubt, I did not wait for food, but fell into a sleep so deep that twenty-four hours passed before I awoke. I then realized with horror that I had only one comrade left. The whole place was deserted and there was nobody to tell us where the Battalion had gone. In a panic Williams and I found our way up the communication trench and discovered with great relief our own company, leaning against the sides, waiting for orders to proceed farther. Our Company Sergeant spoke to us sharply, and we earned the name of 'Shut-Eye Kings'. While we waited each of us disposed of several tins of bully, greatly improved' by the addition of raw onions. After we had satisfied our hunger the order came to advance and, passing from the communication trench into Delville Wood, we were surprised by the security of our transit. That morning the enemy had at last been compelled to retreat beyond the ridge and could no longer fire point-blank at the khaki figures scurrying between the trees. As we jumped over the old front line we saw inside it a number of light field guns which overnight had been emplaced to fire at the retreating Germans on the morning of the attack.

Getting through Delville Wood for the first time without casualties, we were swept by a tornado of angry explosions as we defiled into the open; but in spite of falling figures around us, we kept moving forward, choked by the acrid columns of smoke that climbed high into the air and from within a few yards of our feet. The shells arrived so suddenly that we had scarcely time to flinch, and without ducking pushed onwards to the ridge, where we scattered ourselves along a line of shell craters. Here we waited, looking back towards our former trenches in the Wood and noting the ease with which the Germans had been able to scourge it with machine-gun fire.

Under our eyes a R.H.A. gun team galloped through the wood, coming into action on the fringes of its leafless, shell-torn tree stumps. The German observers had seen it, too, for immediately the first round was fired, a covey of high explosives whirred over our heads, alighting accurately in the form of a cross with the squealing horses in the middle. Two of them were on their backs, hooves lashing the air, and immediately the surviving drivers dismounted to put them out of their pain. Cutting the traces, they galloped home with the remains of their team, leaving the gunners to blaze off over our heads.

The German artillery became irritated and, firing short, found our shell holes repeatedly, so that in a few minutes we lost our Captain and Company Sergeant-Major, as well as many men. We remained in this position, however, until nightfall, when we went forward to relieve the Rifle Brigade in their new line of trenches. We were surprised to find that their attack had taken so much ground, and we marched a long way before we reached a shallow trench in which the survivors were still hurriedly digging. When they had handed over, and were disappearing rearwards, hundreds of skilfully handled miners' shovels were already hard at work, fast tearing chunks of soil from the trench bottom. The Durhams secretly enjoyed digging, and although I laboriously did my share, it was always a source of satisfaction to my miner comrades that they could work more than twice as fast as a mere Southerner. After a while I was sent forward with my section to form a listening post, and a hundred yards in front of our new line I selected a large crater over the rim of which we took turns to keep watch in case the enemy should attempt to regain his lost ground under cover of the night.

Just before dawn we were recalled, finding on our return a deep trench in which rations were being distributed. As we sat eating our thick, buttered lumps of bread and bully, we saw to our astonishment the orderly corporals in the act of distributing a heavy sack of mail. To me came a solid-looking package which, when opened, proved to contain four thick pound-bars of chocolate, sent by a friend for my birthday. Without knowing it, I had been twenty for the last three days, and to celebrate the event I now divided the chocolate among my section. After we had rounded off our breakfast with some of it, we drank deeply from our water bottles, and then noticed that the sky was lightening in the east.

As the dawn broke on 16 September the order 'Fix bayonets' was passed down the trench, and in the wan light we grimly took stock of one another. One young fellow of the recent draft had given a lot of trouble and was already well known for his sharp tongue, but now his face was green with fear so that in noticing him my spirits rose, and when the moment came I leapt among the first over the parapet.

For some minutes we ran onwards without a shot being fired, but gradually a machine-gun or two got to work, making some gaps in the line of running men. By the time our breath grew short the signal came to lie down. Then at the end of a brief pause we raced on, drawing a blizzard of bullets from numbers of fresh machine-guns. Now the fire began to increase in volume, tearing more and more gaps in our line. Our rushes became shorter and faster. We literally dived head downwards to finish each run forward, and, once down, remained motionless, offering as small a target as possible.

After a longer breathing space, completely deafened by the continuous roaring of the machine-guns, I began to look cautiously around, and discovered that my right-hand neighbour, Lieutenant James, was now trying to attract my attention. Even at a distance of three yards, his voice was inaudible and I therefore crept over to take his message. He bawled into my ear 'Pass the word along: are we in touch on the left flank?' and I crawled over with the message to my left-hand neighbour. Before I reached him a bullet went through the brim of my shrapnel helmet giving me the sensation of being hit. Finding no traces of blood, I crept still more carefully to the man on my left, and passed on the message.

Still we advanced, even though our flanks were both in the air, until after a final rush I found myself lying head downwards on the forward slope of a small ridge. Ahead of me, the ground, after dipping for twenty yards, rose abruptly towards a position where I suspected the enemy to be lurking. Beyond this, the ground ascended gradually for half a mile, forming against the skyline a slight eminence on which was the village of Gueudecourt, crowned by the church spire, the aiming point of the attack.

The only man near me was one of our last draft, recognizable by his new khaki uniform. After waiting longer than usual without any sign of fresh activity, I began to take stock of the situation. During the last rush that had brought us to this hilltop I noticed how alarmingly few we had become, and now, fearing we might be alone, I badly wanted to talk to my neighbour. When I hailed him he turned his head sharply rearwards, and to my horror, before he could speak, blood spouted through his hair, and his head sank limply downwards. This example of marksmanship warned me to take care. All around, bullets were angrily whipping into the grass and I wondered how long they could take to reach their small target. Moving so gradually that no observer could notice it, I allowed my head to sink downwards, while, through the bullet hole in my helmet I could see very little immediately to my front.

Every now and then the firing died down, blazing up into an angry continuous roar as succeeding waves attempted to reach the ridge on which I was lying, for following us were other divisions bent on breaking through the enemy's defences. After a time I prayed and fell into a peaceful reverie, thinking of the beautiful years of peace, and the happiness of my old home. What would it matter if this life were ended and I could escape being hunted like an animal, harassed by a perpetual torment of physical fatigue and hardship?

A succession of vivid images, rather like a series of snapshots, passed before my mind's eye, each depicting a scene from my former life. I saw the faces of my parents and of my sisters and, strangest of all, I smelt the acrid odour of printer's ink on fresh sets of galley and page proofs.

Was it then that I began to fall in love with the job which was to be mine for the rest of my working life?

One day, if I am spared, I will revisit that little undulation in the fields between Gueudecourt and Delville Wood on an early morning in mid-September. There I will give thanks for being spared another fifty years of happy and fruitful life to add to the twenty that seemed so likely to end on 16 September 1916.

When after a foretaste of eternity I came out of this daydream, the firing had died down into the desultory snap shooting of snipers with only an occasional burst from the machine-guns. The long rest had brought me not only a wonderful sense of well-being but new courage, and, choosing the moment, I dived head first down the slope into a crater in the valley bottom. As I hurled myself towards it I caught sight of the glittering steel blade of an upturned bayonet, and with my forearm struck it aside as I landed on the unsuspecting occupant of the shell hole. Several bullets zipped into the earth a moment too late, for I was already safely under cover. The owner of the bayonet quickly recovered from his shock and began to beam with pleasure. Poor old Stone, the deaf man, looked as if he had come into a fortune, and his cross old face wrinkled into a broad grin when he realized that, instead of being a prisoner, he had found a comrade. Since his arrival he had kept a sharp lookout over the top of the crater, and he now told me that he had seen some of the enemy withdrawing. We arranged our turns for keeping watch and began to eat our rations and my chocolate. After a smoke I persuaded him to get some sleep while I took the first watch. Just once during this fateful day did we see another of our comrades. Henry, the C.O.'s runner, popped into our shell hole before continuing his journey rearwards. 'The battalion is scuppered', he said.

In the afternoon a whole company of Jagers rushed forward about one or two hundred yards to our right front. I kicked Stone and began firing rapidly over the top of the crater. By the time he had joined me, the dark green figures were drawing level with our position and now they began to falter, falling fast under our enfilading fire. As they worked steadily behind us, each shot winged its man and we kept up the fire until all movement ceased and our ammunition was exhausted.

When we looked at the bottom of the shell hole, there were two or three hundred empty cartridge cases under our feet. Not a shot from the German trenches had come in reply, showing plainly that the enemy had retreated from his position of the morning. After we had watched closely for signs of any survivors we began to realize that we had wiped out the whole company. It seemed strange that no one on the British side had joined in. Clearly we were alone.

Before nightfall a tremendous bombardment was opened up by our own artillery and we soon realized that we were in the thick of it. Shells exploded with terrific concussion quite close to our little crater, throwing up black columns of smoke and chunks of earth. The debris sometimes fell on top of us, sounding more dangerous than it was, as it clanged on our helmets and bounced harmlessly aside. During a terrible hour we buried ourselves into the sides of the crater, not expecting to survive, yet when the gunfire suddenly ceased, we were still uninjured. We then noticed with gratitude that at last the long day was closing.

As soon as we could move safely into the open we went back to the ridge and selected a good place to dig in. Our new position overlooked the front on three sides, and presently we were joined by two or three other survivors who began to help us in digging our strongpoint. We next collected ammunition, bombs, rations and food from the dead bodies, which lay in long lines across the crest of the ridge. Some of the still forms were not quite dead, and through agonized eyes watched our movements as if they knew they were beyond our help. There were so many of them that the task was hopeless, even if we had abandoned our attempt to form a strongpoint before daylight.

Our little band seemed to be the sole survivors of the Battalion. We knew that on both sides the line fell back considerably, leaving us at the apex of a salient, marking the furthest point reached by the attack. Not one of us thought of going back. On the contrary, we collected rations, bombs and thousands of rounds of ammunition and prepared to give the counter-attack of tomorrow a rough time. We had dug our trench nearly waist-deep when approaching footsteps warned us of danger, and with pointed bayonets we waited while two tall figures emerged from the darkness. On challenging them, we discovered the Colonel and Adjutant, who had been searching for the body of the Adjutant's brother, thought to be lying among the attackers on the hillside.

The Colonel's face was set in a bitter scowl as he demanded why we were four hundred yards in front of the Battalion, and as no reply occurred to us we followed the two officers back, wondering why we had been deserted by our comrades. We found them digging a small trench, and learnt that, all told, there were scarcely forty men remaining. We joined them and, digging furiously, began to get warm,

I found that the thought of so many helplessly wounded men lying in front and doomed to lie there all the next day was becoming an obsession, so, seeing no officers about, I called for volunteers. Four men accompanied me back to the fatal hillcrest, where we soon discovered by their feeble moaning a number of still-living bodies. Carrying our first man on his waterproof sheet was stiff work, for the sheet sagged in the middle, so that the corners were gradually dragged out of the grip of our fingers. On our return, four more volunteers joined our party, and we were able to collect fresh casualties, selecting them from the long swathes of khaki figures, mown down by the machine-gunners as the succession of waves reached the crest and melted away. Not all were of our own Battalion, and several of us noticed the badges of other divisions. In addition to those we had placed on waterproof sheets, I attempted to carry on my back a very badly injured man. One leg had been shot away and his cries were too pitiful for me to pass him by. Unhappily the effort caused him such terrible agony that he asked me to put him down and, gently lowering his body to the ground, I promised to fetch assistance to carry him back. Setting off alone, however, I soon realized that I was lost, and instinct warned me that I had walked into the German lines. Suddenly the mist lifted and through the haze of the foreground the church tower of Flers stood out clearly etched in the silvery light of dawn. Turning my back on that light I made off swiftly in the opposite direction until, against the skyline, I caught sight of a line of men walking in single file. Who were they? I went forward with great caution until I could distinguish British shrapnel helmets and then, drawing closer, I discovered my own

Battalion, now the size of a platoon, withdrawing from their unfinished trench.

While I had been away they had been relieved by a battalion of another division, and now in an exhausted condition we followed the Colonel over all those thousands of yards covered by the attack until we again approached Delville Wood. It was a much safer place with the enemy so far away, but the feeling of imminent peril always associated with this baleful place was upon us as we approached its maimed tree trunks and saw the network of old trenches piled with mingled grey and khaki figures to the top of the parapets. Scattered over the former no-man's-land was strewn all the wreckage of war – rifles, groundsheets, bombs, field dressings, haversacks and stretchers; and the mangled bodies of their lifeless owners.

As we looked around us, a stretcher party with its burden was blown to fragments, not ten yards from the head of our tiny column. Pressing forward as fast as we could, we hurried out of this fiendish place, and on leaving it behind, noticed a complete absence of disturbing sound, due no doubt to the withdrawal of the enemy's artillery against the possibility of a further attack.

We halted once more at Pommiers' Redoubt, and at roll call only fifty men were present. These could render an account of but few of their comrades, and the remainder were therefore reported missing. The survivors drew the rations for five hundred men, and for once had more food than they could eat. Everyone had a tin of butter, and as many tins of beans as he liked.

In my bomb bandolier I discovered a bent detonator intended for my liquid-fire grenade, and counted this yet another escape. Very few of us were without marks to show, and most tunics and equipments were ripped by passing bullets. When I heard of the fate of one of our bombing corporals I shuddered, for he, too, had carried a liquid-fire bomb and was burnt to death in sight of his comrades.

As the battalion marched back to Mericourt we passed fresh divisions, with shining buttons and smart uniforms, marching in the opposite direction to take their turn for the first time in the fighting. When these laughing men turned their eyes towards us, their smiles froze on their faces. 'What a bloody battalion!' their expressions seemed to say and they shouted, 'What is it like up there, chum?' We replied grimly 'A bloody picnic', and had a vision of those smart N.C.O.s and officers abandoning their parade manners after a short acquaintance with Brother Bosch.

From time to time the thought of the lines of helplessly wounded men continued to worry me. I knew that now they would be still lying in no-man's-land, cut off from friend and foe, enduring undreamt of agony under this hot sunshine. Perhaps in a week's time a few filthy bundles of rags would crawl into somebody's trenches with dried-up, gangrened wounds and pockets filled with parasitic flies, giving a new division that same loathsome surprise that we received in Delville Wood when a few survivors from the fighting of a week-old battle amazingly reached our trench.

At Mericourt a new Captain, fresh from a rest camp, paraded us for rifle inspection and bullied every man of us for having a dirty rifle. Mine, after so much recent use, was foul, and no amount of gauze on the pull-through would make the barrel bright. Like recruits, we were paraded several times to show our rifles and then we were finally given up in despair. All this switched our minds from the past and we were able to concentrate our bitterness on our unhappy Company Commander.

It has always been a puzzle to me that no officer spoke to us on our return from this battle, or attempted to find out what our experiences had been.

This was not the way things were done in the 29th Division, commanded by General Beauvoir de Lisle, which I was lucky enough to join later in the war.

Chapter 14

Back to Arras

More drafts were hurriedly sent to join us and they consisted mainly of the Derby men who had brought with them their own N.C.O.s. These were made to rip off their stripes, causing us both satisfaction and relief. After the last show I was promised two more stripes, but when one of the bombing sergeants returned to duty I received only one of them. This was thought unfair by my few surviving old comrades and one day I heard Thompson, a dour, grousing, old miner, telling some of the new crowd about our recent experiences. He mentioned my name and, for the first time, I realized I had been adopted by the veterans of the Battalion. From now onwards it was a simple task to have orders obeyed even by the crustiest of old hands.

After being strengthened with reinforcements, we returned to the line north of Arras, where 'A' Company went into reserve at Ronville. Here we slept in the famous quarries, emerging by night for working parties. Later we moved into the support line and led an idyllic life, lazing in the warm sunshine by day and sleeping by night in good shelters. Often I used to leave the trenches without official permission, boldly walking across country into Arras, where a pleasant evening could be spent in the Army Canteen. One day while I was buying some coffee in this cheerful place a sudden bombardment flared up and orders were given for the 43rd Brigade to 'stand to'. Immediately I hurried out of Arras, dashing across country until I reached the support trenches I had left. Fortunately the shelling was more or less confined to the front line, where a German raiding party had collected forty prisoners from the K.O.Y.L.I. under cover of a box barrage. While this was happening I quietly rejoined my comrades, who were manning the barriers blocking the communication trench, which led towards the isolated area of battle.

As usual when our turn came to hold the front line I was out in no-man's-land every night on patrol, but now that few of the experienced men were left it was becoming more difficult to find volunteers for this sort of work. The new officers were keen enough, but they, too, were without battle experience, and it seemed worse than foolhardy to find one of them lighting a cigarette out of bravado when in front of our own firing line. No sooner had he done so than I heard a suspicious noise and, while waiting for something to happen, I took out the split-pin of my Mills hand-grenade in readiness. It was merely a false alarm, but I had a difficult task to reinsert the pin, which I bit between my teeth many times before I succeeded in rendering the bomb harmless. I could, of course, have thrown it towards the German line, but who knows what an alarm the explosion of a bomb would have set off in a quiet sector like this ?

It was when we were resting after the Somme battles that I saw a strange sight. I was the Orderly Sergeant for the Company and as part of my duties I was waiting outside Battalion H.Q. after darkness had fallen. Opposite me was the window of a room so brightly illuminated that I could see our Medical Officer struggling with the mouth of a man seated in a chair. For some minutes nothing the doctor could do with his forceps would disturb the decayed tooth. Then the would-be dentist disappeared and when he returned the shadows of two other men appeared in the window. This time the patient was pulled right out of his chair and at that point the two assistants threw their weight on his shoulders and there in the middle of the room stood the doctor holding up his forceps and displaying the obstinate tooth in triumph. Towards the end of 1916 the 14th Division handed over their trenches at Arras and withdrew for a long rest in the neighbourhood of Avesnes-le-Comte. Soon after we took over our billets in the village barns, I was sent away on a bombing course where, after so many months of trench life, it was a refreshing change to listen to lectures on tactics. Most of the theory seemed simple common sense after our experiences of the Somme fighting, but the new-comers seemed to find it hard to grasp, and the CO. frequently called on me to offer solutions to the tactical problems.

On rejoining the Battalion I found hosts of fresh faces, for another draft had reached us and now the few surviving old hands were completely swamped. When I was acting as Orderly Sergeant I read an order asking for the names of candidates for commissions and my Platoon Commander told me to apply as a means of getting home for a short time, adding that I was just the sort of chap they wanted.

Shortly before Christmas a small party of N.C.O.s bade farewell to their comrades and started off for Blighty, where they were to be turned into officers in the shortest possible time.

The sight of the approaching line of white cliffs awoke a love I had never before known for England. As the troopship crept towards the quayside, we could see a crowd of English faces watching our arrival and their eyes were bright with welcome as we cheered from the crowded decks.

All the common English sights of the landing place had the power to move us intensely. Even the placards and names of stations tugged at the heart strings, adding convincing evidence of reality to what might still prove to be a cruelly deceptive dream. In a fast train carrying us confidently homewards, we caught through carriage windows fleeting glimpses of fields, peculiarly English in their neat hedge-set patterns, of parish spires, screened by wintry trees, rising above the brown roofs of the clusters of cottages and securely tucked away in the peace of England's countryside. After the bitterness of war we were reminded that life could still bring happy days, and our war-locked minds were set free to explore a future where pleasant homely things might have a place.

These sweeping landscapes, devoid of traces of war's devilry, gave us a queer feeling of ownership. Was this, then, our reward for nightly vigils when we had stood on guard, straining into the darkness for signs of the despoiler who menaced the peace of these fair fields and happy homesteads? At least in that hour, our recent adventures seemed worth while and death itself, now immeasurably distant, a fair price to pay for England's immunity.

After a few days at home, I left for Newcastle-upon-Tyne, where at the Depot fresh instructions awaited me to report to the O.C.B. at Rhyl.

At the Officer Cadet Battalion at Kimnel Camp, near Rhyl, some hundreds of N.C.O.s from the Expeditionary Forces were assembling. They were all men who had voluntarily joined Kitchener's Army, and now, after many battles in which they had won their stripes, they had been selected by their commanding officers to undergo four months' training before being commissioned in the New Armies.

They were keen, serious students of the art of war and they were trained by first-rate instructors, some of whom had already won coveted decorations, including at least one V.C. When they finally returned to the battle fronts they brought an entirely new spirit into the ranks of the junior officers. Our lot were ready to lead the conscripts then training to fill the gaps in the units who would be fighting the Passchendaele battles of late Summer 1917.

We all enjoyed the active, varied life at Kimnel Camp, not least because we met there so many congenial companions whose experiences in the different battles were so similar to our own. In our hut there were men from the Royal Naval Division who had fought with it in its first encounters with the German Army in defence of Antwerp. There was one man from the North of Ireland who surprised us with his bitter hatred of the Irish of the South, whom he was all agog to fight when our war was over. Heddle, a quiet scholarly fellow, thought it might be useful to teach us wrestling, and after four 'biscuits' had been placed on the floor of our hut, he overwhelmed us one by one with the greatest of ease. When my turn came round I had the luck to obtain a hold he could not shake and, exerting his great strength, he levered himself over my shoulders to fall inert nearly six yards away on the hard floor of the hut, just missing one of the iron bedsteads. This was a great shock, for the heavy fall shook the hut and for a moment we wondered if he would recover. Fortunately he came to quickly and accepted my apologies in the most gentle manner. Needless to say, we had learnt our lesson and wrestling in an army hut was never attempted again.

Chapter 15

The Twenty-Ninth Division

In the sunny weather of June 1917 I travelled from the Base Camp to the railhead at Poperinghe, taking with me not only the memory of several pleasant swims in the long rollers of Paris Plage but what soon proved useful, some experience in firing my new revolver at Etaples. My one anxiety was the loss of my valise, but this was quickly forgotten when a party of reinforcement officers entered the famous 'Skindles' to order an excellent evening meal before joining their respective battalions.

Considerably refreshed and in fine spirits we later in the evening filed into the street, splitting up into little groups to find our way to various map references. About midnight I located the H.Q. of the Royals and reported myself for duty. Colonel Stevens, a Commanding Officer any man would be proud to serve under, welcomed me in a friendly way and began to ask questions about trench service, following them with a few words of advice. He had himself served in the Durhams as an Adjutant and when a boy he had run away from school to join the Cavalry as a trooper.

Next morning I joined 'Z' Company the Second Battalion the Royal Fusiliers as a Platoon Commander, and took my part in drilling the men. I found that apart from those of my own Company all the subalterns were keen fellows with plenty of trench experience behind them. The Company Captains were mainly old hands with the Division, one or two having won a great deal of respect for their good work in the past. We new-comers soon became sensitive to the spirit of our famous Division, imitating our seniors in their care for the welfare of the men whose interests were considered in every way.

At lunch S – told me that he was 'doomed' to be the raiding officer in charge of the next stunt in the line. He felt incompetent, saying that he did not expect to survive and added that he was the sole support of his widowed mother. Actually he underrated himself for he was to prove a valuable officer before long. Then, rather rashly, I offered to take his place, when he at once became more cheerful, accepting my offer without any show of hesitation.

Before the end of a week we began to move towards the front line, and as the Division was entering the salient for the first time I was sent on ahead to find the route 'Z' Company were to follow. This gave me some practice in using maps and after a time I had a mental picture of our section of the front.

When we reached the battle zone I discovered with chagrin that I was much more nervous under shell fire than in 1916. Fortunately this initial shakiness began to wear off when we settled down in the support trenches behind the other companies who held the firing line opposite a small salient marked on the map as 'Caesar's Nose'. Our H.Q. dugout was not even splinter-proof, consisting of a layer of corrugated iron barely covered with earth. When shelling started it seemed safer in the trench, where I found that the men appreciated a little cheerfulness during a strafe. Even the worst jokes were better than none. Now that the first cold shock of entering the area of screaming violence was over, I felt that I had an advantage over this mixture of battle-weary veterans and raw recruits, for after a long rest my nerves were steady and with my past experience of shell fire I could reserve my obeisances for really menacing sounds.

About tea-time on the first day in these trenches I opened a note from the Adjutant, telling me to report to the Colonel on the canal bank. Accordingly I set off with the returning runner, and we covered the distance at a great pace, finding on our arrival a large elephant dugout in which was a long boarded table, set out in a civilized fashion with cups and saucers and respectably thin slices of ration bread and butter.

After tea the Colonel asked me if I would like to volunteer for a raid, no doubt acting on a hint from my Company Commander, Captain Angell, and we began to discuss the details as soon as I had agreed to take charge of it. It was arranged to ask for about thirty volunteers, but the question of a silent or prepared attack was left open until I had had time to form an opinion by reconnaissance. I therefore went into the front line to get the lie of the land by looking through the Colonel's periscope.

Very little could be seen, apart from the tangled coils of barbed wire and the posts of the entanglements, but one object was prominent several feet above the trench line. This was a flat-topped, concrete dugout marking the nearest point of the German trenches and at the very tip of the salient known as 'Caesar's Nose'. When it grew dark I made up my mind to visit this spot, but my proposed patrol clashed with Benson's and we therefore agreed to go out together. Before we had crept many yards beyond our own wire the air over our heads was filled with the whirring of a Stokes trench mortar bombardment, and a hurricane of bombs descended with angry explosions on the German wire not very far ahead of us. The explosions of the bombs lit up the whole front, providing a thrilling spectacle which held our attention until we were startled by one or two shorts, at which we exchanged disgusted glances, and swore fiercely under our breath. Then, seeing that our patrol must be abandoned before the shorts fell still closer, we climbed back into the trench, no longer holding back our opinion of the people at H.Q.

Next morning I moved back to the canal bank to take charge of twenty-eight men who had volunteered for the raid. As a whole they were a reassuring crowd, including some seasoned N.C.O.s and men of the old sort who volunteered every time for dangerous jobs. Benson, who had joined the 2nd Battalion Royal Fusiliers with me, had volunteered to take charge of the tape. My first move was to ask for a few men to come out on patrol in the evening, and at sundown I led a small party into the front line, where we divided into two groups. Two men were to come with me while the others were to act as a rearguard, remaining behind at some distance from the entrance to our wire entanglements.

Gradually accustoming ourselves to the lie of the land as it showed up under the glaring white light of the German flares, the forward party crept slowly towards the German line, now revealed behind curling tangles of wire and suspicious-looking shapes that, in the light of the flares, proved to be only the stakes of the entanglement.

Scarcely had we reached the enemy's barbed wire than our own eighteen-pounders bewildered us with a sudden storm of shell fire, smashing the wire around us which glowed red hot in the centre of the fiery balls of the explosions. Hot acrid fumes filled our nostrils, as we wondered whether to stay or run. Before we could make up our minds, all was over, and falling back on the reserve party, I was surprised to find every one present. We withdrew into the firing line and as I led the way homewards I made up my mind to report the difficulty of reconnaissance under fire from our own guns.

My report was treated with consideration and the next day Brigadier Jelf, D.S.O., took the trouble to stroll over to my dugout in order to reassure me that next time the gunners would hold their fire between certain hours of the night. I therefore selected another batch of men and, following the scheme of the previous night, crept with two companions up to the German wire, working along it until we arrived opposite the flat-roofed dugout at the point of 'Caesar's Nose'. After watching for about half an hour, I decided to work forward and enter the trench. Indicating my intentions by signs, I left the men behind and crept through the wire until I reached a hole into which I cautiously inserted my feet, crouching as low as possible while I worked my way forward. I was still struggling with the wire underfoot when a Very-light pistol cracked almost under my nose and its released flare soared above me high into the sky. As it illuminated the trench line, I saw a monstrous shadow falling on the now clearly defined, grey dugout wall, not ten yards ahead of me.

It was an eerie moment. Wishing I were still lying flat, but not daring to move a muscle, I distinguished first a dome-shaped helmet, then the face and features of a German soldier whose eyes were fixed, staring upwards at the curving path of the flare as it rose towards the peak of its flight and began slowly to descend towards our trenches on the right.

During this intolerable suspense my revolver pointed towards that unsuspecting face while I waited impatiently for the light to reach the ground, where it blazed in a final spluttering of flame behind our line before dying away. At every moment I expected to be shot, and when after an eternity it was safe to move, I watched the head of the German sink down into the earth before I resumed the safer position of my two comrades.

For some time we stared intently at the German trench, while first one flare and then another was shot into the air at regular intervals, showing that the flarelightman was walking from point to point, firing his pistol to make us think the line was strongly held. Satisfied at last that I had obtained useful information, I withdrew the patrol, afterwards returning to the canal-bank dugouts to write up the night's report.

When I was awakened next morning I learnt that our dugouts had been heavily shelled. Going over to Benson, I found that he had slept through the strafe while the elephant frame of his dugout had been forced down until it was almost crushing the other wire bunk next to his own. We had hardly finished breakfast when the Brigadier arrived to talk over the final plans. He wanted the artillery to put down a box barrage to cut off my sector of the German trench from both flanks and the support line. After last night's patrol I was certain that a silent raid would surprise any occupants of the trench before reserves could arrive. Finding me so confident, he agreed at last to keep the artillery fire in reserve in order to support us if we discovered the enemy in a fighting mood. Before leaving he told me that he had read my report and was astonished by my statement that I had remained unseen during the flight of the flarelight.

Special raiding stores arrived at midday and from these were distributed revolvers, bowie knives, knobkerries, and empty sandbags for souvenirs. Besides these, we all received suits of plain service dress without badges, and in a small package were corks, unfortunately divorced from their bottles, with which our faces and hands were to be blackened.

The sight of these reminders of the approaching adventure aroused considerable excitement among the men, who, during the afternoon, began to entertain us with a regatta. My dugout on the canal bank faced away from the German lines. While sitting at the entrance, reading a book, I noticed on the Yser Canal in front of me a strange sight. Lustily plying two oars, a ruffianly-looking member of my band propelled a rectangular box up and down that ancient waterway. Nails served as rowlocks and shovels were the oars, and when rival craft were launched a naval battle began, cheered by the spectators, who were expecting hopefully that somebody would take the plunge into the black slime of the canal. Unhappily as soon as hostilities began the attackers span round helplessly while the intended victim hastily withdrew out of range.

Having exhausted the fun from the canal, the comic member of my band then perched himself on top of a tree to shout insults over to the German lines in the distance. This prank was going too far; the Germans might see him and I made him come down just in time for us to take cover before the accurate shooting of an enemy battery opened up.

The 2nd Battalion Royal Fusiliers Pull Caesar's Nose: a Trench Raid

After an evening meal at the Brigade H.Q., where we met our Staff Captain Gee (he was to win the V.C. shortly afterwards), followed by kind old Brigadier Jelf's blessing, Benson and I returned to our dugouts to don plain service dress, afterwards blackening one another's faces with burnt cork. Each time the stump burnt my face I retaliated with a hot smear of blackness, and soon our faces were as black as any African's. This painful operation over, we buckled on our revolvers, put bombs and torches into our pockets, and then turned out to make a final inspection of the party before filing into the communication trench.

Our own people were no longer in the front line, having handed over to the Middlesex Regiment early in the morning. Heavy shelling greeted our arrival in the communication trench, but as we crouched into the front line the bombardment died down and we discovered with horror all its sentry posts deserted, so that as a line of defence it had ceased to exist. The Middlesex officers, after they had been turned out of their funk holes, began to put things straight, and then, passing the word along that a raiding party was going over the top, we climbed the parapet and arranged ourselves in front of the wire.

Controlling a large party in the darkness of no-man's-land proved a difficult task, but I had explained my plan carefully beforehand and all went well. Fortunately Benson was there to look after the reserve section, and when I had managed to set the other three sections in motion and had dropped Corporal Green with his Lewis-gun team in front of the familiar flat-topped dugout, I found the right and left clearing parties keeping together fairly well. After we had picked our way through the wire, I jumped down into the German trench, leaving the left clearing section to form a block while I explored in the other direction with six men trooping behind me.

Gingerly I groped my way along the dark trench, working round its traverses, nervously keeping a light pressure on my revolver trigger. In time my eyes saw further into the darkness and soon I came to the dugout in front of which the flarelightman had fired his Verey-light on the previous night. Pushing aside the entrance curtain, I knelt down and crept into the intense blackness of the interior cavern to switch my torch into its mysterious corners. Then with relief at finding it unoccupied, I crawled into the second chamber, where I found nothing beyond a few scraps of paper and with these I returned to my party in the trench.

We now retraced our steps and rejoined the other clearing party. The roles of the two sections were then reversed and when I had climbed over the top to lead the way leftwards, the right clearing party remained behind to form a blocking post covering our rear. In this new direction the German trench bent away from our own front line leftwards until the distance between the two trenches was from two to three hundred yards. Sooner or later we must run into the tenants of the German front line, and with this in mind I pressed on, relaxing a little now that the darkness and the nature of the trench line were becoming familiar. In places our shells had burst accurately, smashing the trench and forming barriers of earth over which we climbed to reach the unbroken portion beyond. At these moments the structure of the defences could be examined, and I saw that they consisted of a series of breast-works, revetted with brushwood fascines. In consequence the trench bottom was dry compared with our more deeply dug and very muddy firing line. Scattered on both sides was a zone of shell craters, so numerous that it seemed odd to find the trench itself in fairly good condition. Possibly German working parties came up at regular intervals to repair the damage caused by our shell fire during these early pre-Passchendaele bombardments.

We had been exploring for some time when we came to a number of small dugouts into each of which I switched my electric torch without discovering any enemy. Time was running out and the thought of its swift passage may have quickened my step, for now the men lagged behind. Listening intently for the sound of their footsteps I saw emerging from the darkness beyond the parapet the black silhouette of one of the enemy running towards me. Automatically my revolver got to work and three shots broke the silence of the night followed by cries of 'Kamerad'. Leaping up from the trench and shouting 'Put up your hands', I covered him. As I approached nearer I could see his hands stuck into his belt, while I realized with some alarm that my back was towards the German trench. Gradually his hands were raised heavenwards and at this moment the rest of the party came hurrying to my assistance. The first two men were sent back to our own front line in charge of the first prisoner. This prisoner safely dispatched, I sat down in the trench with my revolver between my knees in order to reload its empty chambers. Soon after the search had been recommenced I had again lost touch with my raiding party when I heard the quick pattering of many feet. It was a section of men running to the assistance of their comrade. Before very long their figures were silhouetted against the skyline. At that moment I emptied my revolver, wounding and killing one or two, while the rest dived into the trench ahead of me. On this I drew a bomb from my pocket and lobbed it over, following it with a second. Now I was weaponless until I could reload my revolver. As I knelt down and reloaded the rest of my party came up and delivered a fusillade of Mills bombs. I sent them forward to examine the casualties and began to turn out the pockets of the nearest dead German.

Meanwhile a galaxy of multi-coloured SOS flares was lighting up the sky over the German reserve trenches, giving us warning that it was time to depart. I sent the men back to the tape, following to see that they all got away safely. At the tape stood my friend Benson, hurriedly winding it up. He indignantly refused to allow me to wait. 'This is my job', he said. I left him behind with some reluctance and reached our own trench, where Captain Dearden, D.S.O., M.C., was still waiting with a field telephone beside him, ready to summon the artillery to our assistance in the event of a miscarriage of the enterprise. This perfect Brigade Major had won a great reputation with our Battalion of the Royals, and whenever possible paid them unofficial visits during their more dangerous moments. For some time we stood waiting for Benson, while Dearden thought how easily a picked body of men could roll up miles of the enemy's front line on a night like this. He held me back for some time, but when Benson failed to return at the end of five minutes, I went out to discover him still patiently disentangling the tape. He was very annoyed when I tried to hurry him, but before long we were able to climb into the trench where the men were waiting to be led back to the dugouts. Altogether I found I had been exploring the enemy trenches for three-quarters of an hour.

When we arrived at the canal-bank dugouts and the men fell out with their prisoner to have breakfast, followed by a generous ration of rum, I reported to the Brigade H.Q., receiving a warm welcome from the Brigadier, who sent for some tea while he elicited the main details of the night's work. Then patting me on the back, he told me to deliver the prisoner to Divisional H.Q., which was now situated near Proven.

When I rejoined Benson for breakfast we were amused to discover the troops regaling the German prisoner with rum and cigarettes. They had discovered two wounds in the fleshy part of his thigh, and these they carefully bandaged, finding that he was still well able to walk despite his wounds.

We all set off on a long march to Proven and although my blackened face was now streaked with white, people whom we passed stared in astonishment, while a real African was so tickled that he forgot to salute. We were all very tired when I halted the party outside the wooden huts of Divisional H.Q. and knocked up the Intelligence Officer. This gentleman turned out in pyjamas and after staring in bewilderment, laughed heartily, and sent for the A.P.M., who wrote out a formal receipt: 'Received One German Prisoner, signed Captain W. P. Evans, A.P.M.' Having disposed of our spoils, for we had collected shoulder straps and various items of identification from the dead Germans, we now marched into the Battalion transport camp and prepared to wash before getting some sleep in the comfort of camp beds inside a bell tent. Just as we had changed into pyjamas, a messenger brought a note from General Beauvoir de Lisle, D.S.O., ordering Benson and myself to take lunch at Divisional H.Q. Half asleep we began to dress.

On the way to the Divisional Mess the Transport Officer, Harding, who had been with the Royals since Gallipoli, came over to congratulate us on keeping up the tradition of the 29th. Like all the old crowd, he was intensely proud of his famous Division.

The Officers' Mess at Divisional H.Q. was a large room in which one long table ran down the centre, while against one of the walls stood a sideboard on which were dishes containing a rich variety of food. Benson and I sat on either side of General de Lisle and next to me sat the C.R.A.

Presently General de Lisle, who still wore one of the first D.S.O.s, which had been awarded to him as a young lieutenant, and who had won fame in the Boer War, turned to me and said that he had read in Comic Cuts (Divisional Intelligence) that during one of my reconnaissances a German flarelightman had fired a Verey-light within a few yards of me and that I had frozen and waited for the flare to go out before moving. He said fiercely: 'I don't believe it, I wouldn't have done it myself.' When I told him that this was exactly what I had been taught to do when I first went into the line with the Durhams, he said: 'Do you know that I used to command the Second Battalion of the Durham Light Infantry in India? I taught them to play polo and we won the Regimental Polo Cup.' Then turning to Benson he began to speculate on our careers when the war would be over. 'You will both go out to South Africa and grow fruit,' he said. 'That is the life for you. You will never work in a city after this.' For this famous old soldier, this was just another war!

After taking our turn at the sideboard, where we helped ourselves to food, we began to be questioned concerning the events of the previous night, and very soon I chose the opportunity to mention how badly the artillery had timed their shelling when I had been out on patrol. I was informed by the C.R.A. that a lack of co-ordination had existed until I had mentioned the trouble in my reports.

Returning from Divisional H.Q., we now looked forward to a long sleep, but on our return everybody was packing up and we learnt that we must now march several miles to the wood selected by the Battalion as a rest camp. When I got down to it I slept for the record period of thirty-six hours, orders having been given that I was to be allowed to sleep off my fatigue. When at last I was awake the Brigadier visited the camp to deliver a little speech, while my ears burned and I longed to disappear into the earth. Still half asleep, I marched the party away, forgetting the command 'Eyes right!' as I raised my hand to the salute. This, of course, was too much for Captain Boult, our adjutant, who made a suitable comment when he got me alone.

Some days afterwards there was a Divisional march past when I was summoned to parade with the General at the saluting point. Horribly conscious of my new ribbon, I rejoined my Battalion and arranged a celebration in Poperinghe that evening, to which many of my new friends came to wish me luck.

The following day I learnt with some surprise that my raiding party was to enjoy a seaside excursion. Two lorries were put at our disposal and Benson and I took the holiday-makers for a ride northwards to Dunkirk. We amused ourselves by studying the countryside, and as we passed through Bergues the sight of the anglers sitting on the canal bank and watching their upturned umbrellas which served as floats gave rise to much hilarity. At last the lorries stopped in sight of the sand dunes and the sea, and here the drivers asked me for further instructions. Looking seawards I noticed the bleak stretches of sand and in consultation with Benson I decided to put it to the vote – sea bathing or a drink at the estaminet which happened to be just opposite the spot where the lorries had halted. The poll was unanimous, and so we paid for drinks all round and returned from that outing to remember, years later, that the name of Dunkirk was oddly familiar.

Looking back it is easy now to see that the reason for the success of the raid on 19 July lay in discovering the secret of the way the Germans were holding their line by the reconnaissances made on the four nights previous to that of the raid itself. The Germans had planned carefully for our attack on 31 July, and instead of wasting good troops by exposing them to our heavy bombardment throughout July, they withdrew them and arranged to man the pill-boxes (like the flat-topped concrete dugout) only on the eve of our great attack. The success of their plan was reflected in our heavy casualty lists when the battle was under way, for the pillboxes, manned by expert machine-gunners, took a heavy toll in the Passchendaele battle.

Chapter 17

The First Passchendaele Battles

For some weeks the Division now went into training for the approaching battle, and during the intervals we amused ourselves occasionally by visiting the concert party who put up an excellent show, sometimes in a theatre in Poperinghe and at other times in the barns of Proven. This concert party, later known as the Co-Optimists, continued its success on the London stage long after the war.

A subaltern's war was a different affair from the private's war, and one of our greatest pleasures was the cross-country ride to the Field Cashiers to draw the pay for the troops. Borrowing horses from the transport camp, we rode in pairs across fields, skirting farms and always avoiding congested roads. During these rides we regained our freedom, galloping carefree and happy, far off in thought from yesterday's battle.

Towards the end of July 1917 the 29th Division knew that they were to attack with the Guards Division in the same Corps in the hope of breaking through the salient and penetrating to the Belgian coast now held by the Germans. As an accompaniment to the military preparations the skies broke and poured down an unceasing deluge of rain which continued up to 31 July, the date fixed for the attack. On the morning of that day the Guards crossed the Yser Canal at Boesinghe, advancing to the line of the Steenbeck. Here the 29th Division relieved them and my platoon, arriving ahead of the rest of 'Z' Company by several hours, thanks to my prismatic compass, took over from a company of the Guards.

Company H.Q. was handed over by Guards officers, from whom I learnt that during the day a German patrol had been observed approaching the stone bridge crossing the Steenbeck. They had not, however, taken any action themselves. After settling down in the trench I took six men and approached this bridge until I distinctly heard the blood-chilling sound of loud whispering coming from the other side of the stream. This brought us to a halt, while I waited, straining my eyes into the darkness beyond the bridge. After some time I began to think the alarm had been imaginary. With great caution I crossed the stream and climbed the slope on the far side. On the crest of the ridge was a line of trees linked by small bushes and some wire, and when I stood against the nearest of the trees, peering round the trunk with a loaded revolver in readiness, two figures rose from the ground in front of me so that I fired my revolver instinctively. All around figures got up hastily from behind the bushes, and as they made off with the sound of a flight of birds, the men behind me opened up a heavy fire with their rifles. When I stopped to reload my revolver two rifles were rested on my shoulders, the men using my body as a support to steady their aim. In a few seconds the shadowy figures of the enemy had disappeared into the darkness and we vainly attempted to penetrate the hedge to look for casualties, but without wire cutters it was a hopeless task, and disappointed I returned to our trench to write out a report. What surprised me so much was the size of the party that fled so precipitately; there must have been forty or more of them.

When we re-entered the firing line Lieutenant G——, our acting Company Commander, had arrived and expressed his desire to visit our bridge. I took him towards it, but as he approached he remembered with alarm that he had left his revolver behind in the trench, and this reminded me that I had forgotten to reload my own, on which when I mentioned it he turned and fled, afterwards feeling very amused when he recalled that we had gone so far in front of the line without any means of defence.

When the Colonel read my report he sent up orders for me to post a group of men on the far side of the stream. I selected a boxing lance-corporal and his section, and discovered a convenient shell hole above the bridge where I left him and his men feeling rather lonely. I therefore promised to visit them from time to time.

During the short period in this trench there were few casualties in our Company, but both Battalion H.Q. and the other companies sustained heavy losses and we were all glad to return to Proven. On my arrival at the rest camp the Colonel sent for me and congratulated me, promising that the next time I distinguished myself he would recommend me for the D.S.O. He said I could have a bar to my M.C. now if I wanted it.

The 86th Brigade was in reserve for the next attack and we waited in the shell holes east of the canal, while from all sides of the smoking arena gun flashes glinted in the distance like the matches of spectators on a dark Saturday afternoon at Twickenham. With the counter-bombardment falling heavily close by I went to sleep, waking in time to lead my platoon to the newly won position on the Brombeck. Arriving first, I took over Company H.Q. and waited for G——, and the other platoons. When they came up an hour later, G—— sent them into the front line and kept my platoon in reserve. I stayed with him in a small pill-box and in the morning began to explore the line, and crossed over the boundary of the Langemarck railway to get into touch on the right. On the other side of the railway lines I discovered some dugouts and, poking my head into one of them, was astonished to discover a very tall German. I drew my revolver and told him to come out. When he crawled through the low doorway he proved to be a magnificent, athletic fellow about six foot six, wearing on his chest the Iron Cross First Class. Insolently and with supreme indifference he drew himself to his full height and looked over the parapet towards the German lines, probably estimating his chance of reaching his comrades, but when he noticed my revolver pointing menacingly he turned round and walked across to our dugouts, where I found men to take him down the line.

Later in the day the Adjutant arrived with a message asking me to go out on patrol that night with the idea of returning with at least one prisoner. When it grew dark I took a corporal with me and began to walk towards the firing line, when a sudden fierce strafe blinded me with smoke, and in a minute I was knocked over by the concussion of the bursting shells. My companion disappeared and I afterwards discovered that he had turned back, thinking I had been killed. Disappointed at being deserted, I went on after calling for the corporal a number of times, and when I reached the firing line I tried to find volunteers without success. Then in despair I ordered a section of men to come out with me and heard them complaining that they had never been in the line before. One man, however, seemed a stout fellow, and I therefore left the others behind to cover our advance while going forward alone with my untried companion.

We walked several hundred yards, keeping the railway on our right. Then we lay down as a tremendous bombardment began, and over our heads came a great roaring noise of shells speeding to the German positions some hundreds of yards ahead of us. As I watched the shell bursts I noticed the smoke hanging suspiciously about the ground instead of dispersing in the usual way, and in horror realized that we were putting over gas. Since we were without respirators, I decided to remain at a safe distance while watching for signs of movement. None came and presently we turned back, expecting to run into our supporting party, but this had disappeared. At length I noticed shrapnel helmets at the bottom of a huge crater, probably made by a seventeen-inch shell from a naval gun, and throwing earth down at them I aroused the sleeping patrol, who were far too green to be taken on this sort of affair. Almost heartbroken at having had such scanty support, I returned to report my failure to H.Q.

When the battalion was relieved we heard that we were to to go on a course of intensive training in readiness for the next big attack. I received orders to attend a Lewis-gun course at Le Touquet, where I arrived after a long journey without my valise, it having been separated from me by the splitting up of the train.

At Le Touquet everybody was disturbed by the mutiny at Etaples, where we learnt that the overseas troops had fallen foul of the 'Canaries' (the Bull Ring instructors), and were now lawlessly wandering about in large bands utterly out of control. They had no quarrel with fighting officers and during our leisure we went over to Paris Plage every day unmolested by the mutineers for a swim in the long rollers that refreshingly washed away all the recent jarring of our nerves, leaving us braced and fit with minds at peace.

During the Lewis-gun course we were supposed to select tactical positions for machine-gun posts and, after choosing by a series of guesses a dozen or so, I was accused with some indignation of having been on the course before, but in fact I had not. My luck in picking the right position was no doubt the result of battle experience.

After a pleasant week or two I rejoined the 2nd Royals, who were soon ready to move towards the trenches. They marched cheerfully to Boesinghe, and for a few days remained in reserve in an encampment of tents surrounded by scores of other units similarly placed. The enemy was quick to realize that here was an excellent place to drop bombs, for, however badly he aimed, someone would be caught. At night therefore it was not unusual to hear the loud steady droning of aeroplane engines interrupted at intervals by the ear-splitting crashes of falling bombs. On one occasion we saw in the transport lines a score of dead mules, lying on their sides like a row of toys knocked down by a child's missile. As L.G. officer I would turn out in pyjamas, take over from the sentry and then pivot one of the Lewis guns towards the searchlight-eluding black specks, opening up a protecting fire until the Colonel himself joined me similarly clad. Then he would take his turn with the gun. To us it was great fun potting at these low-flying planes.

On 4 October, Wise, the Intelligence Officer, and I were sent up the line on a visit to the Battalion H.Q. of the Dublin Fusiliers, who were engaged in a small nibbling attack to straighten the line for our own coming advance. We went through a zone of heavy shelling and, for my part, I missed the company of the men as we walked towards the attacking battalion with plenty of time to observe the ghastly figures resting in the green slime of the shell holes, and the twinkling flashes of the crowded batteries lining the slopes of the saucer-like depression in which battle was raging.

On reporting to the Colonel of the Dublins we found that the support of our own battalion would not be needed, the attack having been completely successful.

We therefore returned along the duckboard track, timing our passing of the Iron Cross cross-roads by waiting for the regular arrival of three shells among the ruins, and then running past through a cloud of red brick dust until we reached a point a hundred yards beyond. Here we eased up and turned to look round just as another batch of shells fell with precision on the crumbling mound of bricks.

On the eve of 9 October the Battalion left Boesinghe by platoons. Gleaming in the rain, the waterproof sheets and shrapnel helmets of the troops could be picked out in the darkness as we hurried over the canal bridge to follow the guides along the newly made fascine roads leading to the positions taped for our assembly before the attack of the morrow. Benson had been given the task of running out tapes and just before we came to them, Dearden, the Brigade Major, cheerily shouted 'Good luck' as my platoon left the track and began stumbling across the torn fields chosen for the jumping off place.

Captain Angell soon found a shelter and prepared to sleep, but knowing we were not yet in the right place, I took my batman Prentice and tried to discover the other companies, whom I found very difficult to locate in the darkness. During my wanderings I was struck several times by descending fragments of shells which rang sharply against the steel of my shrapnel helmet without doing any damage. Presently, having lost touch with Prentice, I went on and finally learnt where we should be. With this information I returned to my platoon and moved them off. As they climbed out of their shell holes our preliminary bombardment opened up with the crushing violence of a thunderstorm. At the same time day began to break and from all points of the compass the shining bayonets of the attack thrust themselves from innumerable holes in the earth. The men of the 2nd Royals in long files of platoons began their advance towards the enemy, cut off from sight by a long wall of smoke rising from the shell bursts of the creeping barrage.

Behind me the platoon struggled round the lips of shell craters, wholly unable to form into line. Several times I attempted to shout individually into each man's ear to make them form a line, but all I received in reply were bewildered noddings showing that my voice was inaudible in the storm of shelling. To make sure of our direction I stopped now and then to take a compass bearing, but after a time the whole attack had drifted to the right, leaving a gap on the left flank which I did my best to fill without losing touch with the rest of the Battalion, who seemed to be drifting too far to the right.

On reaching some higher ground I had a good view over the top of the barrage, and a mile away could be seen the edges of the Houlthurst Forest, towards which a long straight line of men moved as if on parade. These were the Guards, and I thought that if they were covering ground similar to ours their great prestige was well deserved. Our people were either advancing in small knots, or, like my own platoon, strung out in crocodile formation. When the barrage halted we all jumped into shell holes.

Thinking the halt a good opportunity to sort out my platoon, I left the shell hole and had started to collect them together when a bullet tore through my wrist. Feeling it go limp I went back to the stretcher-bearer, seated coolly behind our line of shell holes with three or four men sitting beside him waiting to have their wounds bandaged. While I waited the blood poured out fast from the severed artery and it looked as if very little was left of my right wrist. Taking my turn, I felt the iodine poured into the gaping hole and after the bandage was tied I grew very faint, but I was still able to rise to my feet and walk to a shelter where a couple of stretcher-bearers removed my equipment and gave me a drink from a water bottle filled with rum.

Stimulated by the drink, I was able to walk back to the first dressing-station, dodging the counter-barrage that was now in full swing. Here I fainted as the injection was thrust into my left arm, and after a short rest in the adjacent waiting-room, I was carried out to the first motor ambulance that arrived, soon afterwards reaching a casualty clearing station, where I was given an anaesthetic.

When I awoke in the CCS. it was evening and the marquee was nearly in darkness. I discovered that I was in bed and in hospital pyjamas. At the end of the bed I saw Benson leaning forward on his chair, and when he saw me awaken he told me the latest news of the attack.

Next morning Benson, who had been lightly wounded, had gone and after breakfast I followed him down the line in a hospital train that carried me to Le Touquet.

My shattered right wrist took me home to Blighty, where I thoroughly enjoyed my spell in a wonderful ward in King's College Hospital, Denmark Hill. It was full of young fellows with pretty severe wounds, and when Captain Lascelles arrived with the first news of the

Cambrai tank battle we celebrated his V.C. in the Florence Restaurant, thanks to the brilliant organization of the Ward Sister, who managed to transport the whole lot of us from Panchia Ralli Ward to the West End.

Then came a longish spell in Eastbourne at the Command Depot, where we continued our massage treatment and built up our physique by playing games in the afternoons. Meanwhile, things were looking very gloomy on the other side of the Channel. Reading the newspapers, we watched that dreadful map of the bulge day by day, wondering how large it would grow before our comrades were separated from the French.

Of the two thousand young officers at the Eastbourne Command Depot, most had received bone injuries which required massage treatment; otherwise they were physically fit and spent any portion of their mornings left over from their treatment in attending the usual parades and lectures. In the afternoons they were encouraged to play games, and duties were excused for those who went to the tennis club in Gildridge Park to play tennis with the members who at that stage in the war were all women. Although even by early May I could not hold a tennis racket securely, I did my best to hit the ball on those delightful afternoons away from it all. I had by then discovered that one of the local dentists could be a valuable aid to the enjoyment of sea-bathing and a pleasant morning on the sea front. In those days there were no army dentists and my teeth after years of neglect sadly needed attention. I therefore took advantage of another privilege arranged by the Commandant of the Command Depot and attended the dentist's surgery with some regularity until pretty well all my teeth were loaded with lumps of metal filling. The daily dental treatment over, I struck out for the sea front, where I found my friends ready to spend a carefree morning listening to the band. Afterwards we would hire an old-world bathing machine which was trundled into the sea so that we might descend its little ladder into reasonably deep water, just like King George III at Weymouth a hundred and fifty years earlier,

One day I saw a pathetic sight. Four men on crutches hopped down to the water's edge, where they threw their crutches aside and plunged into the sea. Although each had lost a leg they all swam well and did not seem in the least handicapped by being short of one of their limbs.

It was at Eastbourne that we first came across the Americans, for our girl friends who were staying at one of the hotels on the sea front quickly deserted us to dance with a party of American officers who had just arrived. Later I saw a picked body of American troops all of whom must have been six foot six inches, beside whom our own Guardsmen would have looked quite short. This was a sight to bring great comfort to their battle-worn allies.

When at last I appeared before a medical board and was told that I should be marked in a category for Home Defence, I begged the old men to let me return to France. They were quite startled and then one of them said very graciously: 'Well, my boy, if you want a V.C., we will mark you AI when you come back in a fortnight's time.'

However, although I had my way, it was quite a long time before I had to report to Dover, and in the meantime I enjoyed some leave and found time to attend an investiture at Buckingham Palace where King George V pinned my medal on my chest and said 'Brave fellow' in what seemed to me a rather guttural voice.

Before I left Eastbourne I took part in a relay race at a Sports Day held in the grounds of Eastbourne College. My squadron had the best team, with the exception of myself, and the hundred yards sprinter gained a fine lead which was increased by the two-twenty yards man. By the time the quarter miler handed over to me, I found myself a good fifty yards ahead of my rivals. Alas I was no runner, and with another lap to go I was on the point of being overtaken. Then the crowd decided that my squadron must win, and I finished with a sprint that just scraped me home in the lead. However, when I arrived, I found that I was muscle-bound, and I was popped into a hot bath to recover.

About this time I was approved on medical grounds for training as a pilot in the R.F.C., but I did not bother about this idea. I had at last received orders to report to our Depot at Dover. During my examination by the R.F.C. doctors it was observed that I habitually altered the position of my chair before sitting down. This singularity, for some reason unknown to me, gave rise to much discussion.

Chapter 18

I Join the 13th Battalion Royal Fusiliers

My stay at Dover was short, and after I had enjoyed the bathing at Paris Plage while waiting for the customary period of twenty-four hours for my various inoculations to take effect, I found myself travelling in the comfort of an ordinary compartment, so unlike the cattle trucks of my first journey, to join my unit now far in advance of the trench line of my earlier days. It was an exciting journey, for my companions kept on pointing out famous landmarks, the scene of desperate battles of the previous years. We were winning the war and the reefing was beginning to dawn on us that it would soon be over.

No nicer crowd could have been found than the 13th Battalion, a territorial unit which formed part of the 37th Division. They were now nearly at the end of a long war and casualties had been replaced time after time with men of the New Armies. Even so, something of the old friendly spirit of the territorials remained and I had every reason to be pleased with my welcome. The Colonel at once made me Intelligence Officer and put me in charge of H.Q. Company. This gave me the pleasure of accompanying him on his reconnaissance of the position we were to take over on the west bank of the Scheldt Canal south of Cambrai. I was astonished to find how the war had changed, for we were able to stroll in the open without any need for concealment, although we could see quite plainly the enemy positions on the rising ground on the opposite side of the Canal. While planning our dispositions we ran into a group of Australians who were manhandling some captured field guns and loading them with ammunition to fire the shells point-blank at the targets on the rising ground opposite us. This wonderful example of self-help has always remained in my mind as typical of the Australian and New Zealand infantry.

On October the 8th the 13th Battalion was ordered to take part in the Second Battle of Le Cateau and overnight my job was to synchronize watches. On my return I was told to get some sleep in the wooden shelter which was our temporary Battalion H.Q., for next morning I was expected to find a forward H.Q. and to keep out of the attack. When I awoke I found myself alone and I walked towards the advancing waves of the Battalion, hoping to see on my way a suitable site for H.Q. Alas, my enthusiasm ran away with me, for I soon caught up with the front waves of our attack and found everyone lying down, held up by the fire of just one machine-gun on our right flank. It struck me that I should work my way to the company on the left to suggest that the CO. should envelop this enemy position, and as I braved the machine-gun fire a half-dozen times I was unlucky enough to be hit once more in my right arm without having made any contribution to our advance.

Here was another compound fracture, this time in the upper part of the arm. If I had not been quickly disentangled from my useless arm and bandaged by a plucky stretcher-bearer, I might have lain long in a helpless state on the ground. As it was, I could walk back to the first-aid post and from there I was quickly transferred by a Red Cross van to the Casualty Clearing Station. By the time I had enjoyed three weeks in hospital at Boulogne the war was in its final stages.

In the Autumn of 1918 my experiences of the previous years were repeated fairly closely. In 1917 my right wrist was shattered by a bullet in a dawn attack on 9 October. Now once again I was crossing the English Channel in a hospital ship, and about to continue my treatment in another hospital in England. This year the bullet that shattered the upper part of my right arm was fired at roughly the same hour in the early morning and just one day earlier in the month of October.

As I lay in my comfortable bed in the hospital train after we had been disembarked and were on our way, I wondered if I could possibly be so lucky as to be unloaded at London a second year in succession. It was therefore a very cheerful hospital patient who was carried by four elderly stretcher-bearers to an ambulance destined for the Prince of Wales's Hospital in the Old Central Hotel at Marylebone.

I should find it hard to imagine a more comfortable or a happier place for a young wounded officer than the spacious ward in which I now found myself. One or two more operations, however, were still ahead of me before the long splint suspended above the bedclothes was discarded, and I was equipped with a somewhat handier Thomas splint on which my arm was stretched to allow the missing four inches of bone to grow. It was with this cumbersome equipment that I was allowed to take my first walk out of hospital on 11 November. Sharing the growing feeling of excitement around me, I was soon drifting towards Trafalgar Square, where I arrived in time for the official announcement of the signing of the Armistice at eleven o'clock in the morning.

Until that moment I had not begun to realize what an important landmark in our lives had been reached. Indeed, as little by little the excitement around me seemed to increase, I was at first mainly concerned that someone should not knock into my large splint, but my fears were quite groundless and everyone courteously gave me a wide berth.

Soon lorries carrying munition workers began joy-riding through Trafalgar Square, the passengers dancing on the floors of the lorries and screaming at the top of their voices. Alas, I could not share their high spirits, for the new life which was now beckoning had involved an enormous sacrifice, and would be yet another challenge for those like myself who had had the good fortune to survive the perils of the long war. Surrounded by people whose experiences had been so different, I felt myself a stranger and I was lost in thoughts they could not possibly share.

Later in November, Sister Cooper, who so efficiently ran our ward, arranged for a few of us to be entertained by members of the Royal Automobile Club. An old gentleman drove four of us to Richmond Park in his car along roads almost completely free of traffic and then, after pausing a few minutes to gaze at the trees, he brought us back to Pall Mall. Two of us sat at a table in the Club with a charming old lady who poured out tea and entertained us. She told us that many of the officers who had been captured by the Germans early in the war were about to come to the Prince of Wales's Hospital to continue their treatment, and this would mean that we should soon be allowed to live at home and to attend the hospital as outpatients. It was only as we were leaving that someone whispered in our ears that our kind hostess was Princess Marie Louise.

It was not long before we found out that the Princess was right, for the ex-prisoners of war began to fill the ward and it was a pathetic sight to see their legs suspended in long splints above their beds. The Germans might have done their best to set their fractures, but, alas, all must be done again if the bones were to be straightened so that these unlucky men might walk normally at long last.

Once the news was spread that some of us would be able to live at home there was great excitement; a few of the more fit began to leap over a bed that had been pulled into the centre of the ward. I had just exchanged my Thomas splint for a much smaller one and like a fool I tried to jump, only to catch my foot at the top so that I crashed down on to the floor on my wounded arm.

What was I to do? I got up and walked out of the hospital to spend a miserable day away before returning shamefacedly to have my arm looked at. When our astute and kindly R.A.M.C. Colonel examined me he looked hard with his keen grey eyes and then, turning to the Sister, snapped: 'Get him ready for another operation immediately.'

Looking back half a century later I realize now that those five years which began for me on I September 1914 were not sheer loss. During them I had grown to manhood, and when I was demobilized in June 1919, at the age of twenty-two, I had learnt in a hard school a number of valuable lessons which affected my career in many ways during the next forty-five years. But, as this narrative shows, I was one of the luckier ones. Many of my comrades were not only wounded more frequently, but had to pass through much greater ordeals before returning to their peacetime tasks; others are to this day in hospital, as cheerful and courageous as they were in their youth. We who were so fortunate when we came 'To the long way's end at last' will never forget the other million of our comrades.

Glossary

Archies	Anti-aircraft guns.
'Blighty'	A wound necessitating hospital treatment in England with some leave afterwards.
Bull Ring Instructors	Base Camp Instructors responsible for drilling newly arriving reinforcements.
Canaries	*see* Bull Ring Instructors.
Fascines	Faggots made of brushwood, used to line or lay on the bottom of trenches.
High-Lows	Soldiers' boots.
Poilus	French foot soldiers.
Rookies	New recruits, young and inexperienced soldiers.
Shorts	Shells, fired by our own gunners, which fell short of the target or pre-determined line of barrage.
Whizz-bangs	Low trajectory field guns firing usually at almost point-blank range.